Three Ugly Sisters

A Biblical Exploration
of Covetousness, Jealousy, and Envy

By C. E. Hastie

RESOURCE *Publications* · Eugene, Oregon

THREE UGLY SISTERS
A biblical exploration of Covetousness, Jealousy, and Envy

Copyright © 2022 C. E. Hastie. All rights reserved. Except for brief quotations in critical publications or reviews, no part of this book may be reproduced in any manner without prior written permission from the publisher. Write: Permissions, Wipf and Stock Publishers, 199 W. 8th Ave., Suite 3, Eugene, OR 97401.

Resource Publications
An Imprint of Wipf and Stock Publishers
199 W. 8th Ave., Suite 3
Eugene, OR 97401

www.wipfandstock.com

PAPERBACK ISBN: 978-1-6667-4754-6
HARDCOVER ISBN: 978-1-6667-4755-3
EBOOK ISBN: 978-1-6667-4756-0

VERSION NUMBER 101722

Cover artwork by Kristien Harris: harris.myportfolio.com

All scripture quotations (unless otherwise stated) are from The Holy Bible, New International Version. Copyright © 1973, 1978, 1984 by International Bible Society. Used by permission of Hodder & Stoughton Ltd. All rights reserved.

Scripture quotations marked "KJV" are taken from Holy Bible, King James Version.

Contents

Acknowledgements | vii

Introduction | ix

1. Covetousness | 1
2. Potential Effects of Covetousness | 12
3. Some Suggestions for Dealing with Covetousness | 23
4. Any Good Things about Covetousness? | 35
5. Jealousy: Joseph and his Brothers | 42
6. Judah | 49
7. Jealousy: Leah and Rachel | 57
8. Dealing with Jealousy: Human Perception Verses Spiritual Reality | 67
9. Any Good Things About Jealousy? | 77
10. Envy: The Destroyer of Joy | 81
11. Envy: Saul | 87
12. Envy: The Pharisees and Sadducees | 96
13. Overcomers of Envy: Nicodemus, Joseph, and Paul | 104
14. Some Suggestions for Dealing with Envy | 113
15. The Evil Eye | 119
16. The Evil Eye: Through a Glass Darkly | 126
17. Gleanings | 132

Bibliography | 141

Acknowledgements

With thanks to family members: Stephen, Aimee, Sarah, Steve, and Kristien, who helped with advice, encouragement, and support, as well as much needed technical help and design input.

Thanks to friends: Amy, Colin, Fi, Geoff, Heather, Jim, Joy, Karen, Margaret, and Mariska, who variously read the text, advised, corrected, encouraged, and most importantly prayed. Thanks to you all, mainly for just being the wonderful people that you are!

In addition, thanks to all the patient, kind, and efficient staff at Wipf and Stock.

May God make His face to shine upon you all.

Introduction

I have called these conditions "Three Ugly Sisters" to emphasise how closely linked and interrelated they are. Indeed, the words used to describe them are often used interchangeably, especially envy and jealousy.

They are also very ugly in nature; so ugly that often people don't want to admit to having a problem with them - even Christians!

For the purposes of this book, I have tried to tease them out one from another to be able to examine them in closer detail and get a clearer understanding of each condition.

I have completed a section on all three of these "sisters" looking at: definitions; at least two Bible accounts that aid our understanding for each one; other Bible verses that may be relevant; how to deal with these emotions/conditions; and is there anything good or useful about them? There is a final section on the "evil-eye." Though related it is not quite the same.

All Bible quotes will be from the NIV, but I will state when other translations are used.

I would like to emphasise here at the beginning of the book, that most of the contents are based on notes from my own private Bible studies. I write with this in mind and would like you to bear this in mind too.

We should all complete as much Bible study as we can and be prepared to check these things out for ourselves. I am not claiming a particular authoritative word on the topic and am merely offering up my thoughts here for your consideration.

If you disagree or feel I have misrepresented something I hope that it will lead you to complete your own studies and come to your own conclusions prayerfully, with the help of the Holy Spirit.

Thank you for reading and may God bless you.

1

Covetousness

Cinderella

Most people are familiar with the story of Cinderella. She is a beautiful girl who is oppressed and bullied by a wicked stepmother and two ugly sisters. She is eventually freed from her life of slavery by a prince with the supernatural assistance of a fairy godmother. This is a tale that is known across ages and cultures sometimes with slightly different characters and storylines. The universal story it tells is of someone rising from the cinders of the basement to the rich and fulfilled life for which they were always destined. You could say it was an account in which someone receives "beauty for ashes." It is a universal story because it expresses the desire of most people to follow the trajectory of Cinderella, to escape from imprisonment and be truly free. This is possible. It is possible with the help of the son of a king and some supernatural assistance too.

People who are not Christians, and sometimes those who are, can have quite a warped view of the Bible and the God of which it speaks. They see the Bible as a dour book full of rules, forbidding them to indulge in all the good things of life, and God as a stern master, ready to rap them over the knuckles the minute they step out of line. Nothing could be farther from the truth. God wants to free you from all the things that are oppressing and crushing you both internally and externally. To help you to be the person He always intended. "To bestow (on you) a crown of beauty, instead of ashes" (Isa 61:3).

He has written a book that will help us find the way to our proper home and be that fulfilled self, and everything He tells us to do in that book is with our very best interests at heart. He wants us to be free to be eternally beautiful. Perhaps if previously your view of God was of a demanding and authoritarian master and His "rules" as restrictive and joyless, possibly it will help if you look at the situation differently.

The Bible is not really a rule book; it's an escape manual!

The Three Ugly Sisters: covetousness, jealousy and envy are just some of the things that may keep us imprisoned, living in the ashes of broken lives. There are of course others too. This book is an attempt to discover what the manual has to say about how we can be delivered from these three, particular, jailors.

Covetousness

In conversations today covetousness is a word that is hardly used. Most people will never have heard it uttered and certainly not used it themselves. This may not seem to be such an issue, after all language changes over time and "old-fashioned words" are often consigned to the dustbin of history. However, terminology is important to help us articulate a concept. The totalitarian government in George Orwell's novel "1984" were aware of this fact and were trying to reduce the language to its most basic form believing that, without the appropriate word, ideas they viewed as undesirable, would be impossible to express. It was just one route that they took to keep a large population of potential rebels in check.

If a word cannot be eradicated from the language, then another avenue to explore is to change the definition or redefine it, so that far from seeing something as a problem, we can be trained to see it as a beneficial quality instead. Today we are encouraged to covet, though of course the word itself is not used. Indeed, nearly every advert our eyes behold are enticing us to covet. Without covetousness where would our economies be? Therefore, it is important as Christians that we keep both these things in mind as we study this subject. We need to be aware of the word and what it really means and realise that it is not a virtuous or even harmless attitude but a sin.

The so-called deadly sins are all fully represented in the advertising with which we are constantly bombarded: lust, envy, greed, sloth, pride. The conditions upon which we are concentrating, I have called the three ugly sisters, to emphasise how closely linked and interrelated they are. Indeed, the words used to describe them are often used interchangeably, especially envy and jealousy. This confusion of terms and concepts can mean that it is not only hard to define them but also to deal with them. They are also extremely ugly in nature and therefore even Christians often do not want to admit that they may have a problem with them. The aim of this book is to attempt to look at these "sisters" separately to come to a clearer understanding of them individually. Then examine various Bible accounts and verses which may serve as a way forward in dealing with these damaging attitudes.

The Eyes Would Have It

Words and definitions are of course an important starting point and therefore an appropriate place to begin. The Hebrew word that is interpreted as covet is:

> *Chamad* (verb): to desire, take pleasure in.
> It is variously translated as: attracted, covet, coveted, delight, desirable, desire, desired, desires, pleasing, precious, precious things, took great delight[1]

Looking at these various alternatives and noticing how it is used in scripture we see that sometimes it is employed in a positive way and sometimes negatively. This is of course dependent on the rest of the verse in which the word is contained and considers the motivation of the person involved and upon what their desire has rested. The obvious verse that would come to mind for the negative aspect of this quality would be the tenth commandment in Exodus 20:17: "'You shall not covet your neighbour's house. You shall not covet your neighbour's wife, or his manservant or maidservant, his ox or donkey, or anything that belongs to your neighbour.'" It is good to desire or take pleasure in some things and we shall consider this at the end of this section but here we are being warned not to desire that which belongs to someone else.

The first appearance of this word in scripture is Genesis 2:9: "And the Lord God made all kinds of trees grow out of the ground—trees that were pleasing (*chamad*) to the eye and good for food." God was pleased, took delight in, all He had made and if indeed He was going to covet anything it was indeed all His to covet. It was legitimate. To covet what belongs to someone else is not.

1. Strong's Hebrew Concordance, 2530

The second appearance of this word comes shortly after, in Genesis 3:6, when we read regarding The Fall: "When the woman saw that the fruit of the tree was good for food and pleasing *(avah)* to the eye, and also desirable *(chamad)* for gaining wisdom she took some and ate it."

The Hebrew word *avah* is also used here which is practically synonymous with *chamad*. Indeed, in Deuteronomy 5:21 both words are used in the reiteration of the tenth commandment. In themselves neither *avah* nor *chamad* denote anything necessarily bad. They are expressing a strong desire. It is what the desire rests upon that can cause the problem. We all can look at things and take pleasure in them or even desire them and leave it at that. It is when this desire gets out of control that the problem begins; when it starts to reside in us and begins to consume our thoughts. Then it becomes idolatrous. We may then begin to take action to try to obtain the thing or person we covet with no regard to consequences.

Achan's Sin

A biblical example of this would be the account of Achan in the book of Joshua. When the Israelites entered and destroyed the city of Jericho, they were told that all the silver, gold, bronze, and iron were to be devoted to the Lord. They could take nothing for themselves. Achan, disobeyed this command and when his sin was uncovered, he said this: "'When I saw in the plunder a beautiful robe from Babylonia, two hundred shekels of silver and a wedge of gold weighing fifty shekels, I coveted them and took them. They are hidden in the ground, inside my tent, with the silver underneath'" (Josh 7:21).

Sometime a covetous desire takes years to come to fruition. Sometimes it happens in a moment of disobedience as here. He had been clearly warned along with everyone else to take no plunder, but he chose to disobey. This had horrific consequences not just for him but for his family and his community. The Israelites lost a battle and men were killed as a direct result of this sin and Achan lost his own life along with the lives of his whole household.

Wasn't this rather harsh? Were his actions so terrible?

Of course, firstly, and most importantly, he had disobeyed a direct and specific order of God. It also demonstrated a very flawed understanding of God and His powers. A God who is omniscient is not fooled by any hiding place. In fact, regarding our conduct before God, there is no hiding place. "Nothing in all creation is hidden from God's sight. Everything is uncovered and laid bare before the eyes of Him to whom we must give an account" (Heb 4:13). This New Testament verse would not of course have been known to Achan but he had just seen a demonstration of this attribute of God in the destruction of Jericho prior to the incident which proved to be his downfall. For example, God had known about Rahab's views and exact whereabouts and was completely capable of directing the spies to her home in a large and unfamiliar city. In addition, within living memory, God had saved Achan's people from slavery stating: "'I have indeed seen the misery of my people in Egypt'" (Exod 3:7). These are examples of God's omniscience. Everyone else had obeyed the direct order but not Achan. The reason he gives was that he "coveted" the items. Whose items was he actually coveting? They had just been told that all the devoted items belonged to God. He was coveting what belonged to God and stealing from Him.

Covetousness can lead us in a wrong direction physically, morally, and spiritually. It can lead to theft, bearing false witness, adultery, idolatry and even murder. In fact, to breaking practically all the other commandments. The desire for the item or person can be so overwhelming that it causes us to lose all sense of perspective and responsibility and just give in to our desire.

The account of the aftermath of Achan's sin in Joshua chapter 7 emphasises the damage that an individual sinner can do to one nation, tribe, clan, or family. One man from the tribe of Judah causes this problem. Eventually another man from the tribe of Judah will put all to rights. An echo of the first Adam and last Adam situation. It is noticeable that God treats the Hebrews as a corporate solidarity: "'They have taken . . . they have stolen . . . they have lied'" (Josh 7:11).

We are responsible for our own sins, but we are also our brother's keeper.

We are not told in the text, but I wonder what would have happened if after the defeat at Ai, Achan, had gone to Joshua and confessed his sin rather than waiting to be called out in this inevitable way? "He who conceals his sin does not prosper but whoever confesses and renounces them finds mercy" (Prov 28:13). Perhaps he could have redeemed a little of the situation? We will look at this element in more detail in the following chapters.

You Shall Not Covet

Looking back at the original commandment as written in Exodus we are told not to covet people or possessions. Regarding possessions, we are specifically told not to covet our neighbour's house, ox or donkey or anything belonging to him. In Achan's and Eve's case they both took what they had coveted. We may not necessarily do that. Indeed, it will probably be impossible for us to do so. However, just the act or the set state of coveting has a detrimental impact on our spiritual and mental health and even potentially our physical constitution.

In the commandment coveting someone else's wife is also forbidden. The implication being that you look at your wife and then look at someone else's and compare and contrast—and the comparison is unfavourable. It could be for many reasons; looks, personality, ability or even the material and monetary benefits she may bring to the marriage. You think someone has been given a better deal, and, in an earthly sense that could be true. Someone else's wife is bound to have some attributes that yours does not. We are all individuals and are good at different things. We have different abilities, skill sets, and personalities. However, possibly there are a few things that you are not considering.

Firstly, we are very good at seeing the flaws in those nearest to us because we live with them and every day their faults are ever before us. The opposite is also true, because we are so close to them, we often forget to appreciate their good points too, or more likely, just take them for granted. Whereas we see the object of our desire through rose tinted glasses, the reverse is often the case regarding our actual partner, we see all their bad points and none of the good.

Secondly, we are overlooking the part that God plays in this scenario. If God is omnipotent and omniscient and the Bible tells us He is, how could you be married to the wrong person? Of course, no marriage is perfect, and all marriages will have problems, sometimes terrible and difficult problems, but that does not mean you have married the wrong person. If you are a Christian and prayed about the decision you made, or to be honest, even if you didn't, then you are married to the person God intended for you. The fact that you are not happy with it now and are looking elsewhere, has really nothing to do with it. This is of course setting aside obvious exceptions such as adultery.

Your main commitment as a Christian is to God and your second is to your spouse. That day after day encounter which comes from living closely with another person is going to greatly assist God's aim in reforming your selfish nature. Naturally, you are not happy about it. Your flesh is crying out for ease and pleasure. Yet if you quit in this arena of marriage, you will not free yourself of this process, it will merely continue in another relationship or another area of your life—and it may even be worse. If you have decided to give up on God's purpose for your life and make a life of pleasure and ease your focus, then that is a different matter. Jesus told us that before we become disciples we should "count the cost" Luke 14:28. God will do the work He wants to do in us and through us, one way or another, and if not through marriage, it will be another way. He picks the best way for you individually. Your role is to stick at it, to persevere. Not bail out to run to pastures that look greener.

Even if you do not act on the covetous desire that you have, if you do not deal with it, it will have a detrimental effect on your marriage. A constant comparison of your wife, or husband, with another in your mind is going to colour your relationship with her or him, especially when it is an unfair and unrealistic comparison. It will also affect your relationship with God because you are not dealing with a real situation in the real world, you have moved into the realms of fantasy and imagination.

I am aware that many people can have very difficult marital situations and unsurprisingly enough so is God. In fact, He is more aware than anyone. He can also change things if He wishes. He can change you and He can change your partner too. More will be said about this at the end of this section which has some ideas about dealing with covetousness.

However, what if you were not a Christian when you got married and have since become one, but your partner has not? I am sure that those of you in this position are very familiar with this verse from 1 Corinthians:

> To the rest I say this (I, not the Lord): If any brother has a wife who is not a believer and she is willing to live with him, he must not divorce her. And if a woman has a husband who is not a believer and he is willing to live with her, she must not divorce him. For the unbelieving husband has been sanctified through his wife, and the unbelieving wife has been sanctified through her believing husband. Otherwise your children would be unclean, but as it is, they are holy.
>
> But if the unbeliever leaves, let him do so. A believing man or woman is not bound in such circumstances; God has called us to live in peace. How do you know, wife, whether you will save your

husband? Or, how do you know, husband, whether you will save your wife?
(1 Cor 7:12–16).

This is a very hard position in which to be, but the advice is quite clear. Some people have had to live this for years and can testify to its sound reasoning, as well as how painful it can be. Apart from that, it is the word of God! We have already seen in Achan's story what happens when we decide to disobey God. There is a very colourful proverb which says: "Better to live on a corner of the roof than share a house with a quarrelsome wife" (Prov 21:9). This is an acknowledgement of how difficult a situation can be.

If you are finding this section particularly painful to read, you should take comfort in the fact that God knows only too well how awful this situation is for you. If you turn to Him daily and work with Him, He really can help resolve even the most seemingly dire situations. He can help with strength for the day and hope for tomorrow.

The Power of Love

Something that may assist a little is to consider the idea of love that we have in our society today. The way we talk about romantic love is to speak of "falling" in love as if it is something unavoidable, something we are unable to resist. We suffer some confusion of understanding in the English language because we only have one word for love. The New Testament was written in Greek which has four words that are translated as love. A knowledge of them can really aid our understanding. They are:

Storge: familial affections, as a parent for child
Philia: the love we have for friends, platonic love.
Eros: romantic or sexual love
Agape: an act of will. Doing the right thing even when we don't feel like it.

Agape is a love which can be commanded. It is the love God has in mind when He tells us to love our neighbour or indeed our enemies. We cannot necessarily command our affections in this regard. It is unlikely that initially we will have warm, friendly, feelings towards our enemies, but we are to do the right thing by them regardless: feed them if hungry; clothe them if necessary; pay back evil with good. We can decide to do the right thing even when they are doing the wrong thing.

It is easy to see that covetousness knows nothing of this type of love. Coveting if anything is based on eros, in other words, lust. When we say we have fallen in love with someone who is not our spouse we usually mean we have fallen in lust with them. We have promised to love our spouse in the bad times and the good. It is not an additional extra or something we do until we meet someone better or someone that we prefer. In this instance you are not so much falling in love as deciding to stay in love.

The commandment specifies coveting someone's wife it does not mention husband. Is this because the fair sex does not suffer from the sin of covetousness or never covets another woman's husband? Of course not. The commandment is telling us not to covet another person's spouse. However, whilst we are examining this element it is very interesting that it does specify only a spouse regarding family relationships. Imagine if it read: you are not to covert another person's mother, daughter, son, or uncle. Why spouse?

You cannot change the other relationships even if you wanted to. Your mother is always going to be your mother. It is a fact of reality. We may "adopt" other family members: consider and treat someone else as our mother or father, but we cannot change the physical fact of the original family relationship. You don't covert someone else's mother because you can't. You covert someone else's wife because you can. Or, rather, you think you can. In fact, the marriage relationship is as set in stone as the parent/child relationship. It is till death. You have become one person. The fact that we covert someone else's spouse demonstrates our flawed view of marriage, as well as the hard reality of married life on occasions.

Another relationship that is referred to is: "manservant or maidservant." Not many people today have man or maid servants but some of you may have employees and colleagues. These are people that we may have to deal with and work with consistently day by day. You can spend more time with these people than you do with your own family. They can make your life easy or very difficult. It is just as wrong in God's sight to covert someone else's work mate as to covert their spouse.

I Want It

Finally, possibly not many of us are coveting our neighbour's ox or donkey but the fact is that we should covert nothing whatsoever that belongs to our neighbour. Not his car, garage, or boat. Or her house, clothes, or hair.

The first commandment and the last are diametrically opposed. The first commandment speaks of the existence of God and by extension our duty towards Him and obedience to His will. The last commandment is trying to show us that what we really want is the opposite. The first commandment is about putting God first. The last commandment is about not putting ourselves first. We know we cannot serve two masters.

The English word to covet is defined as: to long to possess, especially what belongs to another; to inordinately desire, or lust after, without regards to the rights of others. This is not loving our neighbour. It is not loving God. It is not even loving our enemy. It is loving ourselves.

Jezebel—An Enabler

The next biblical example to examine is the account of Naboth's vineyard which is to be found in 1 Kings 21. You may like to read the whole chapter through before you continue with this book. I will refer to and quote specific verses, but it would be helpful to have a grasp of the overall account before you continue.

Here we see that King Ahab's state of mind obviously fits the definition of covetousness that we have just explored. He longed to possess what belonged to another without regard to their rights. Hopefully, when we are tempted to sin, our spouse can be relied upon to help us to overcome this temptation. Unfortunately, in this case Ahab's wife, Jezebel, aided and abetted him in committing the sin. I am not sure we could accuse Jezebel herself of covetousness, but she was certainly guilty of breaking most of the other ten commandments. I mention this case because here we have one person suffering from covetousness and another person carrying out the coveter's desire. There is a very unhealthy form of co-dependency in this relationship as described in 1 Kings.

You may be familiar with the term "Jezebel Spirit" which is used generically to describe a situation where a weak man is controlled by a strong woman. Usually, the man is in a position of power and the woman wants power and seeks to gain it via attachment to, and control of, the man. Certainly Ahab, made no objection to her plan. He did not even enquire how she proposed to acquire the vineyard for him. It was probably music to his ears just to hear her say that she would get it for him. Coveting, like lust, consumes. It consumes our better judgment. It consumes and obscures all right judgment so focussed are we on the object of our desire. It blocks out all else from our view. It is an obsession. An overwhelming desire that will not rest until it is satisfied. Fortunately, most people are not in the position of power that Ahab and Jezebel were to fulfil their passion.

The irony is that often when we finally get the object of our desire, we find it turns to ashes in our mouths, especially when it has come at the expense of another. We may come to despise or hate it. We see this in the account of Amnon and Tamar in 2 Samuel 13. Amnon lusted after his half-sister Tamar. He plotted and schemed and eventually raped her. Then we read this: "Then Amnon hated her with intense hatred. In fact he hated her more than he had loved her" (2 Sam 13:15). His lust now satisfied turned to hate.

Even in historical events nearer to our time we can see this scenario played out. King Henry VIII lusted after Anne Boleyn for eight years. He put aside and eventually divorced his wife. He overthrew convention; the church of the time; destroyed worlds and individuals to have her. Once his lust was consummated, rather like that of Amnon before him, it turned to hate and after a few short months he had her executed. She may have received a reprieve had she bore him a son but that was nothing to do with his passion for her but his passion for a successor. Covetousness and lust are closely related.

In this chapter we have looked briefly at some definitions of covetousness and some biblical examples. Now we want to consider in more detail what effects this sin can have in all areas of our lives.

2

Potential Effects of Covetousness

Not Accepting or Cooperating With God's Plan for Your Life

The Greek word used in the New Testament for covetousness is:

> *Pleonexia* the definition of which is advantage, covetousness
> Usage: covetousness, avarice, aggression, desire for advantage
> A word derived from *pleion* which means numerically more and *exo* which means: desire for more; lusting for greater number of temporal things that go beyond what God determined is eternally best for you; beyond His preferred will.
> From *pleonektes*: avarice (by implication fraudulent, extortion, greediness.)[1]

We see here an explanation of one of the roots of the problem. God has a plan for everyone's life. It may not be easy or problem free, but it will be a good plan. He has even determined the place and time in history that you will live, with the sole purpose of enabling you to see the gospel, and then begin to fulfil the purpose for which you were created:

> From one man he made every nation of men, that they should inhabit the whole earth; and he determined the times set for them and the exact places they should live. God did this so that men

---

1. Strong's Concordance, 4124. https://biblehub.com/greek/4124.htm

would seek him and perhaps reach out for him and find him, though he is not far from any one of us" (Acts 17:26–27).

Though God has a scheme for your life you will still need to cooperate with Him to bring this to fruition. Covetousness means firstly, you have not accepted this fact. All our earthly lives we will struggle with elements of God's plan. We may find it too hard; too slow; too boring; too difficult. Often, we find the narrow path too narrow and look at the beautiful pastures through which we are passing and want to wander off for a little while. Our flesh calls out to us to do this. The definition from the Greek text describes how we want to go beyond what God has determined is best for us or even just faster than He has determined is best for us. Someone else's dwelling may look much more comfortable and luxurious; their wife more amenable and beautiful; their job, even their role in the church, more prestigious and fulfilling, but you must remember God has a design for you, and it's for you alone, and it will not be the same as his plan for anyone else. You probably do not know what is best for you. You don't even know yourself very well. As the old hymn says, you need to trust and obey.

Therefore, one of the first effects that covetousness may have is to take you away from God's plan. His preferred will for your life. It additionally may mean that you have not accepted He is in charge of your life completely: all of your life, every single aspect.

Reinterpretation of Bible Verses

Perhaps there is something that your covetous desire is urging you on to acquire, or something it is coaxing you to do, but you know that the plain teaching of scripture forbids this action. For example, as we looked at earlier, the Bible says that a married believer should not leave an unbeliever if the partner is willing to stay. This can be a very hard road to follow, leading to years of difficulty and strife. Therefore, you may be tempted to look askance at this passage of scripture and look for other ways to interpret this verse. This re-evaluation could take some very plausible routes. After all, you may tell yourself, this scripture was meant for a different time, a different culture, and how could a generic rule be made to apply to such individual circumstances? You perhaps covet a different lifestyle, in this case possibly a believing partner, and therefore start to look suspiciously at some Bible verses. The force of covetousness can enable its grasping hand to undermine even the authority of the Bible itself.

Additionally, you may start to listen to the world more than God, telling yourself: people do fall out of love; you deserve a good life now; this is the only life you will have, and you must make the most of it. Perhaps, even more perniciously, fantasising how much more you could do for the Lord with a believing partner, or whatever it is that you are coveting. You may even start to believe this propaganda whilst forgetting from whom it really originates.

There are many, many things that the world will tell you that you want to hear. Remember the devil comes as an angel of light. He can look good, enticing, and beautiful, holding out offers of endless, wonderful, opportunities that don't exist on this boring, narrow, hard, road upon which God has set you. However, if you run away from the grindstone that God is using to change you, He will find another one to use; that is if you want to continue in your relationship with Him. "Beware of turning to evil which you seem to prefer to affliction" (Job 36:21).

God will continue with our sanctification during our lifetime, and it will probably be painful at times, but we need to remember: "we also rejoice in our sufferings, because we know that suffering produces perseverance; perseverance, character; and character hope. And hope does not disappoint us. . ." (Rom 5:3–5).

There are many other examples that could be used to show how we may begin to reinterpret Bible verses to enable us to fulfil our own desires. Only one example has been given here, but the underlying principle remains the same.

May Make you Stingy and Ungenerous: Coveting Money

The tenth commandment clearly tells us to covet neither people nor possessions. Money would be a good example of what is referred to in this regard. We may covet money and that can lead us to be very mean and stingy, even with the portion of money that belongs to God.

"Therefore I thought it necessary to exhort the brethren, that they would go before unto you, and make up beforehand your bounty, whereof ye had notice before, that the same might be ready, as a matter of bounty, and not as of covetousness" (2 Cor 9:5 KJV).

The attitude in which you give your money does matter. You should not give your money grudgingly but with a generous heart, not allowing your spirit to be infected by covetousness. God loves a generous hearted giver! This is the mindset of which He approves. It is quite clearly associated with righteousness in many passages in the Bible.

An overwhelming desire to accumulate money or goods can in turn effect your willingness to tithe or give money to the work or people that God would like you to support. It may become harder and harder to part with the money you know should be dedicated to the Lord and His work. It becomes a tug of war between the I that is coveting and the Spirit that wants us to give generously. If you do notice this happening to you then that could be a sign that covetousness is getting a grip. As in everything in Christianity we are to be sensible and achieve a balance. We do not really serve God's purpose if we give everything away and make ourselves paupers, dependent in turn on others. As Paul says "it is the *love* of money that is the root of all kinds of evil" not money itself.

Money is something that we should use. It has no intrinsic moral quality, neither good nor bad. It is our inner desires that cause the problems. "For the love of money is the root of all kinds of evil: which while some coveted after, they have erred from the faith, and pierced themselves through with many sorrows" (1 Tim 6:10 KJV).

Notice how serious the situation can become. Paul speaks of people having wandered away from the faith. Showing that when this covetous spirit gets a grip in our lives it wants to be in charge and craves its own way. If it masters us, then we have become its slave.

"They promise them freedom, while they themselves are slaves of depravity—for a man is a slave to whatever has mastered him" (2 Pet 2:19).

Covetousness Makes us Unclean

We can see here in this quote from Mark what Jesus thinks about coveting (greed). He is referring to what is in our heart:

> He went on: "What comes out of a man is what makes him 'unclean.' For from within, out of men's hearts, come evil thoughts, sexual immorality, theft, murder, adultery, greed, malice, deceit, lewdness, envy, slander, arrogance, and folly. All these evils come from inside and make a man unclean" (Mark 7:21–23).

Jesus is clear about what thoughts are evil in this extract. Here He is talking to the Pharisees about their notions of clean and unclean; pure and impure. In this passage the word *pleonexiai* is translated as greed and is seen as an unclean thing. We find the same word and implication in Luke 12:13–15:

> Someone in the crowd said to him, "Teacher, tell my brother to divide the inheritance with me."
> Jesus replied, "Man, who appointed me a judge or an arbiter between you?" Then he said to them, "Watch out! Be on your guard against all kinds of greed; (*pleonexiai*) a man's life does not consist in an abundance of possessions" (Luke 12:13–15).

Jesus' answer here to the disgruntled brother seems odd, partly because He will eventually be the judge of all people and situations. But perhaps the real thrust of Jesus' reply was to make the brother consider the wider context of judgement and turn his focus from earthly inheritance to spiritual matters?

The man's request seems fair. We don't have much information but to divide an inheritance would seem the right thing to do. Jesus turns from the brother's question to address the crowd and take the opportunity to warn them about greed. Jesus' response, and the parable which He uses to illustrate His point, really demonstrates very little interest in the temporal situation of inheritance at all. He was not commenting on the brother's situation in the here and now, but urging him, and everyone listening, to consider the much more important matter of their eternal future. Temporal things are just that—temporal.

Immediately after the brother's request Jesus tells "The Parable of the Rich Fool." The main character in that parable died on the very night in which he acquired his greatest wealth. He took none of his earthly wealth with him.

> "But God said to him, 'You fool! This very night your life will be demanded from you. Then who will get what you have prepared for yourself?'
> "This is how it will be with whoever stores up things for himself but is not rich toward God'" (Luke 12:20–21).

If you are going to be greedy about anything, then make sure you are greedy about the things of God. An unhealthy obsession with an accumulation of wealth makes us unclean in God's sight.

Potential Effects of Covetousness

Makes us Concentrate on Earthly Matters to the Detriment of our Spiritual Progress

The next appearance of covetousness that we will consider is in Paul's letter to the Romans.

> "Furthermore, just as they did not think it worthwhile to retain the knowledge of God, he gave them over to a depraved mind, to do what ought not to be done. They have become filled with every kind of wickedness, evil, greed and depravity. They are full of envy, murder, strife, deceit, and malice" (Rom 1:28–29).

This section begins with:

> "The wrath of God is being revealed from heaven against all the godlessness and wickedness of men who suppress the truth by their wickedness, since what may be known about God is plain to them, because God has made it plain to them" (Rom 1:18–19).

You are probably very familiar with this chapter, but it would be beneficial to read it over, so you can follow Paul's train of thought and see how the chain of depravity that he describes here develops and continues. It begins with godless people who suppress the plain truth of God. Leading them to think it not "worth while retaining the knowledge of God." Covetousness, the big I of the Ten Commandments, the I who eventually comes to be in opposition to God, can in a worst-case scenario, eventually lead to this terrible situation where we may become like unbelievers who suppress the truth and don't think that the retention of the word of God is worth the effort. This suppression of truth may start in a small way but as Paul is trying to show in this passage it can lead to a sharp acceleration down a very slippery slope.

Christians often talk about belief and unbelief as two separate and distinct states of being but even as committed Christians we can have areas of unbelief; things that we find hard to accept or don't want to accept, especially if it involves a sacrifice. We know our flesh does not like sacrifice. In addition, we are a work in progress, not the completed article, so we must grow in belief as in other areas of our life.

If we allow this spirit of covetousness to grow, it can lead us further and further away from God. Its very nature is greed and therefore it will consume as much of our life as it can if we don't deal with it biblically.

Impatience with God's Timing

What about spiritual things? It is possible to covet someone's spiritual gifting and ministry. I think we would do well to consider in this regard, that God wants to grow our character as well as our gifts and in fact it is essential that character grows alongside our gifts. If you are training someone to use a powerful tool or attribute you need to make sure they have the character to handle it well. A soldier will be trained to handle a gun, how to use it, maintain it and shoot well. However, alongside that practical instruction will go coaching concerning how and when to use this lethal weapon as well as being taught the discipline of doing everything correctly.

You would not hand a five-year-old a loaded gun. They are too immature. God cannot give immature Christians powerful tools or gifts. In the Christian world maturity is not necessarily linked to time, some people can be immature after thirty years as a Christian, and others quite mature after three. It is a fruitless and potentially dangerous pursuit to covet something that you are ill-equipped to handle. Imagine the damage that five-year-old could do with a loaded gun!

It is true we are told to covet spiritual gifts, but the timing of when, or if, these gifts will be given to us, or when we will have chance to operate in them, is out of our hands. We want to rush the programme, leap a few steps, miss out some of the boring training. Covetousness wants its demands met now. It doesn't want to wait five or ten years. It is in tune with our fast-food, quick delivery, cannot wait, society. Our desire for spiritual gifts needs to be balanced alongside patience with God's timing for their bestowal and application.

The Covetous Roots of False Teaching

The passage below from 2 Peter shows another route that a covetous spirit may travel. It may be a main motivating factor for false teachers. The desire for money may be combined with other equally damaging cravings including the selfish impulse for spiritual attainment and power. The Bible warns us many times about this situation.

> But there were also false prophets among the people, just as there will be false teachers among you. They will secretly introduce destructive heresies . . . In their greed (covetousness) these teachers will exploit you with stories they have made up (2 Pet 2:1–3).

Later in the same passage, Peter, still talking about false teachers: "With eyes full of adultery, they never stop sinning; they seduce the unstable; they are experts in greed (a heart they have exercised with covetous practices KJV)—an accursed brood!" (2 Pet 2:14). The motivation of these teachers is power and greed. They are going to exploit the flock for their own ends. It will probably be mainly for monetary gain, but it could also be for sex, control, power, and the adulation that a position may bring. Notice Peter says they will exploit you with stories they have made up. How do we know that they have made up a story? An obvious clue would be if they are encouraging us to do something that the Bible forbids or does not encourage. Or if they are suggesting that they have some extra or secret revelation. We are warned not to add or subtract from the word of God. False teachers are often more in-tune with the spirit of the age than the word of God.

The Bible assures us that if we are truly seeking to obey God we will not be deceived, or at least not for long. On the other hand, if you are deceived it could be because you want to be. You are deceived with your own consent. God is much more willing to tell us the truth than we are to hear it. The Bible speaks of our itching ears. We can look for a teacher that tells us the things we *want* to hear not the things we *need* to hear. False teachers not only have a wrong motivation themselves, but they can lead others down the same path.

Discord Within the Fellowship

Not only may covetousness cause us to wander away from the faith or community of Christian fellowship, but it can also lead to much tension and discord amongst the fellowship:

> What causes fights and quarrels among you? Don't they come from your desires that battle within you? You want something but you don't get it. You kill and covet, but you cannot have what you want. You quarrel and fight. You do not have, because you do not ask God. When you ask, you do not receive, because you ask with wrong motives, that you may spend what you get on your pleasures (Jas 4:1–3).

James lists a raft of problems here. Not merely quarrelling and fighting but killing also. All these issues arrive from passions within us and the greed which is driving us on. It is quite shocking to realise that James here is talking to the church. The battle rages within the individual themselves.

The believer's flesh is at war with the indwelling spirit. This inner conflict, if not dealt with, spills out into open conflict within the church. James continues by emphasising once again, that friendship with the world is enmity towards God.

Notice also, another impact of covetousness is mentioned here; it can critically affect our prayers. We can pray with a covetous motive, that we may spend what we get on our pleasures. The god of hedonism which is one of the chief gods of our world who wants us 'to eat, drink and be merry', is seated right here, squatting in the middle of our prayer life. We are asking God Almighty to provide us with money so we can go and spend it on another god. Would you say yes to a prayer with that motivation at its heart?

We see here that covetousness can cause internal conflict for the believer, and potentially impact their prayer life, as well as causing friction within the church.

Pride of Life

What is behind the desire of many in the world to accumulate masses of money and possessions? Only a small minority of people in the world are super rich but often they still seem to want more. They are never going to be able to spend such a huge amount as they already possess in a hundred lifetimes. Sometimes it seems money is just an end in its-self. However, it is what money can acquire that is the real driver: power, independence, security, a life of hedonism, or even a person they desire that they feel may be captured by a particular lifestyle.

The novel "The Great Gatsby" contains a very good example of this type of behaviour. The story centres around the obsession of Jay Gatsby, for a particular girlfriend from his past, Daisy. He desperately covets a relationship with her but also desires the lifestyle that she represents too. His excessive accumulation of wealth and goods were merely the route he took to try to achieve his aim. Perhaps a desire to associate with a particular set of people may also be a motivator?

Probably all the things just mentioned could be summed up as the "pride of life." "For all that is in the world, the lust of the flesh, and the lust of the eyes, and the pride of life, is not of the Father, but is of the world" (1 John 2:16–17 KJV). Pride. The desire of the I writ large. The desire to be the richest, cleverest, most powerful, most beautiful . . . the desire to be the most.

Idolatry

Covetousness can lead us to some terrible destinations and states of being from which we may have revolted earlier in our Christian journey. "For this ye know, that no whoremonger, nor unclean person, nor covetous man, who is an idolater, hath any inheritance in the kingdom of Christ and of God" (Eph 5:5 KJV). Here in the letter to the Ephesians we see Paul state very clearly that no covetous man will inherit the Kingdom of God. We can miss our eternal destiny if we are entangled with this sin of covetousness. How much more serious could it be? In this verse we see an explanation of why covetousness is so injurious to our spiritual health. It is in fact a form of idolatry. What does the Bible mean by the term idolatry? It would seem to comprise anything or anyone that comes before God in our heart. God belongs on the throne of our lives and there is no room for another. Neither will He share with another. We will see much more discussion on this when we come to the next section of this book on jealousy, where this topic will be looked at in more detail.

Another route idolatry may take infecting and derailing our thinking can be to encourage us to focus on one aspect of God's character to the detriment of others, or to the exclusion of others. An example of this in practise can be found in the making of the golden calf as recounted in the book of Exodus.

The Hebrews were fearful. Moses had been up on the mountain for many days and showed no signs of returning soon. His physical presence was very important to their sense of safety. They wanted a tangible entity that could alleviate the fear they were feeling and make them feel secure and protected. The golden calf was an attempt to focus on one element of God's character: His strength. It was also possibly a harkening back to Egypt and a familiar idol from that country. However, God is not a one-dimensional god. Of course, God is strong. He is omnipotent. However, He is also a righteous God: a holy God. The Hebrews here were focussing on His strength and not holding that alongside other equally important aspects of His character. They would find this out to their cost as you can read in Exodus chapter 32. From this we can see why it is important we do not attempt to make an image of God because we could never hope to capture His entirety, and if we, like the Hebrews, were to try to do so, it would be a flawed and marred representation of our own desiring and construction.

Currently, within much of the church we seem amenable to promoting God to the world as a God of Love, whilst at the same time, averse to acknowledging He is also a God of holiness, righteousness, and wrath. If we do not explain the wrath of God and its foundation in our sinfulness, then how will people truly comprehend how loving He is? You really need to grasp one before you can appreciate the other.

We can bolster our idolatrous impulses by only reading, studying, or expounding the passages in the Bible that tell us what we want to hear, and avoid those that remind us of other aspects of God's character with which we would rather not engage. You must not make an idol the commandments tell us. That means we must not make an idol that presents a lopsided God who is not the God of the Bible at all. The writer of Ephesians links covetousness and idolatry. I think we can see why from the examples we have considered. The fearful Israelites desired a visible god. They resorted to idolatry to assuage this desire and paid the price.

We may covet a god who is not the real God of the Bible because it plays to the spirit of the age, or something in our own soul which does not want to accept elements of His nature which we may view less favourably. We must accept the whole counsel of God as Paul tells us in Acts 20:27. "All Scripture is God-breathed and is useful for teaching, rebuking, correcting, and training in righteousness, so that the man of God may be thoroughly equipped for every good work" (2 Tim 3:16–17). The scripture to which Paul is referring as breathed by God is the Old Testament. Surely, all Christians would want to be thoroughly equipped for every good work? Especially if your role is going to be to teach or be a Pastor responsible for reproof and correction. We cannot, as some do, focus exclusively on the New Testament to the detriment of the Old. Who would read only a quarter of a manual and think that they had all they needed to begin to understand and operate a complicated machine?

Here we have considered some of the effects of covetousness. This is not a comprehensive list and there will be other aspects that have not been covered. However, from this short study we see that covetousness detrimentally impacts our relationship with God and with others. It is the complete opposite of the attitude of Jesus. It is a poison to church unity and fellowship, and it damages us too. It is a huge blocker to individual spiritual development and sanctification. Our attention is stolen and diverted from God onto ourselves. It defies and ignores the will of God. It's heartbeat and mantra is indeed: 'I want . . .'

3

Some Suggestions for Dealing with Covetousness

It's a Sin: Name, Confess, Repent

The society in which we live sees covetousness as a way of life and we have probably been infected by that way of thinking too, so the first step is going to be admitting that it is in fact a sin. God thought it serious enough to make the Ten Commandments. It is not an optional extra. We have been told, by God: "You shall not covet . . .". (Exod 20:17).

Repenting, which is how we begin to restore our relationship with God, just means that we agree with His way of seeing things. What He calls sin, we should also call sin. The Holy Spirit will help us in this regard by convicting us of this flawed attitude. God does not deal with all our issues at once, it would be too traumatic and difficult, but gradually He starts to work on the sanctification process. He may deal with it at a stroke in His mercy or it may be something with which we struggle all our lives but firstly we need to recognise that it is a sin.

Naming it, bringing it out into the light, has the attribute of making it real. Whilst it is unnamed it can lurk hidden in the recesses of our mind and spirit. Once it is known and named, we have the choice to ignore that knowledge or, with God's help, deal with it. Possibly talking the situation over with a mature Christian friend that you trust would be an excellent place to begin. Once you have admitted it's a problem then God can begin to work.

Obviously a second step would be to pray and ask God for revelation on how best to tackle the matter. You will probably need to do this frequently, and hopefully with growing revelation and freedom.

This is probably as far as any formula can go because God does us the courtesy of treating us as individuals, and there is no one-size-fits-all. This attitude itself can create as many problems as it solves. You will need to listen carefully to what God says to you individually and put that into practise with His help and guidance. What follows is a list of suggestions that you may find helpful.

Reaffirm a Belief in God's Providential Care and Omnipotence

All our emotions and desires, our whole personalities have been contorted and twisted out of alignment by the Fall. Sanctification is really God trying to put all these things back in good order. In the previous chapter we saw that coveting was wanting more than God thought was good for us, at least at a particular moment in time. Or wrongly desiring what belongs to someone else because you perceive it to be better than something of your own. Therefore, it stands to reason that one of the "remedies" for covetousness would be trying to be satisfied and happy with what you already have, and the position in which you find yourself at any given moment. Paul says about this attitude:

> I am not saying this because I am in need, for I have learned to be content whatever the circumstances. I know what it is to be in need, and I know what it is to have plenty. I have learned the secret of being content in any and every situation, whether well fed or hungry, whether living in plenty or in want. I can do all this through him who gives me strength (Phil 4:11–13).

It can be helpful to consider what is the opposite emotion or state of the sin with which we are struggling so that we can better understand it and deal with it. The opposite of the condition of covetousness would appear to be contentment. If you are content that means you are in a state of peaceful happiness, a state of satisfaction. You need nothing. A picture of contentment is a sleeping baby: at rest; secure; all its needs met. I believe all these factors come into play in order that we can be content.

Covetousness in our heart means we are not at rest, certainly not mentally or emotionally. We are probably constantly thinking of how we can acquire the thing we covet and striving to make it so. Just the mental energy expounded thinking about the object of our desire is tiring. Neither can we be very secure. If we covet it means that we feel something is lacking, either in quantity or quality. This makes us feel insecure and needy. Possibly even fearful that someone has more than we have or is having a better time.

Focussing on peaceful sleep we can see an example of this in the book of Acts. Not a baby in this case but a grown man facing a painful execution in the morning. When capital punishment was still carried out in England it was customary for two warders to stay in the cell overnight with the condemned man. Many of the warders hated this role because often the condemned man was so terrified that he could not sleep; he became incoherent and often lost control of his bodily functions. No sleeping pill was given.

In this incident in Acts 12 the apostle Peter is facing execution in the morning. The apostle James had already been "put to death with the sword" (Acts 12:2) so Peter would have been under no illusions as to what his fate may be. On this occasion Peter was miraculously released from prison by an angel. We read this: "Suddenly an angel of the Lord appeared and a light shone in the cell. He struck Peter on the side and woke him up" (Acts 12:7). Far from cowering in terror, Peter, was so sound asleep that the angel had to strike him to wake him up. That is an amazing picture of peace and trust, in extremis.

Paul says he "had learned" to be content in all circumstances. It had possibly been a journey for him too. His contentment seemed to reside in a deep faith in, and knowledge of, the character of God. He knows God is omnipotent, omniscient, and omnipresent. If you truly believe all these things about God, then how could you not have what is right and good for you at any given moment? Possibly one of the deep roots of covetousness is related to an area of unbelief in your life. You do not believe God is powerful enough or cares enough or has paid enough attention to you to have everything covered. He may have missed something. You may need to do this thing for yourself. Maybe asking God to assist you with more faith would help. We may echo the father of the sick child who said to Jesus: "I do believe; help me overcome my unbelief" (Mark 9:24).

There could be many reasons why you have this deep-rooted attitude. Maybe your early experience of parenting was that your needs were not met. Possibly your parents may have been absent, or you may have been spoilt and had every whim catered for. You may even have had the best childhood imaginable. Covetousness seems to be a part of everyone's nature whatever reasons we use or excuses we give. However this attitude of covetousness has developed, does not really matter, the fact is—it needs to be dealt with. If you develop cancer because of genetics or because of your own cigarette smoking, it still needs to be treated, and blaming something or someone else will not help. If you have repented to God the Father, believed on Christ His Son, and received the Holy Spirit then you are a new creation. You are still a work in progress, but you have been born anew. The way God deals with our past is not the same as the world's.

One technique that the world uses to ignore sin is to rename it. "Woe to those who call evil good and good evil, who put darkness for light and light for darkness, who put bitter for sweet and sweet for bitter" (Isa 5:20). Recategorize covetousness as something more palatable, perhaps self-fulfilment or gratification, and the problem is no longer a problem! The sin is no longer a sin.

One reason for developing a covetous attitude may be that we have lost faith in the fact that God has a plan for our lives, or merely that He is taking too long in bringing the plan to fruition. Perhaps we may never have had that understanding in the first place. We need to firm up on the idea of God's providential control and rest at ease, knowing that He does have everything in hand no matter how difficult our situation may seem and no matter how we may desire to assist Him to speed the progress. How to do this?

Bible Study with Emphasis on the Whole Counsel of God

Memorising relevant Bible verses is an excellent way of retaining God's word and a great help in changing your thought processes. For example:

"The Lord will fulfil his purpose for me" (Ps 138:8).

"There is no wisdom, no insight, no plan that can succeed against the Lord" (Prov 21:30).

"I have hidden your word in my heart that I might not sin against you" (Ps 119:11).

These verses are affirmations of God's care and omnipotence. In memorising them you are taking captive the damaging thoughts you may have and replacing them with spiritual truth.

Examining the lives of characters in the Bible and looking back over your own life will help you see how God has protected and guided you. Remind yourself of these facts, whilst at the same time remembering that sometimes like Job and Joseph, we don't always realise why some things happen till years later, and sometimes we may never know.

We may be coveting because our thinking has become more in line with the things of the world than the things of God. Therefore, consistent, regular, and in-depth Bible study is essential. You can do this with a small group, but it is important you also complete some by yourself too. This is an important factor for our whole spiritual and emotional health. You need to be soaked in the word of God. A short ten-minute devotional, reading one Bible verse and then two pages of someone else's thoughts on that verse is not going to cut it in the long term. Extensive and thorough Bible study takes time and that is something of which everyone seems to be short these days. However, is that really the case? How much time do you spend on your phone; on social media; watching television. There is nothing intrinsically wrong with any of these things and you do need to catch up with friends and relax but if you can make time for these things surely you can make time for God?

We live in a world full of various types of media sources and devices with thousands of voices clamouring for our attention every minute of the day, and most of those voices are at best ambivalent about God and at worst openly hostile. These voices are in our ears and head all day, every day. A short, unsatisfactory "encounter" with the word of God once a day and a couple of hours on a Sunday is not going to be enough to counteract the tsunami of chatter and propaganda trying to sweep you in the opposite direction. If it is your desire to know more of God and His word, I believe He will help you find the time. Either way you must find the time, if you want to stay spiritually healthy and grow.

Distractions

Examining the incident of the visit of Jesus to the home of Martha and Mary you can see a very valid point being made in this regard (Luke 10:38–42). Martha was in the kitchen, working hard to get a meal ready for everyone. Mary was sat at the feet of Jesus listening to Him. Martha was doing a very important thing; everyone would need to be fed and after all she was hosting Jesus Himself. She came to the Lord with a complaint and asked Him to tell her sister to help.

> But Martha was distracted by all the preparations that had to be made. She came to him and asked: "Lord don't you care that my sister has left me to do the work by myself? Tell her to help me!"
> "Martha, Martha," the Lord answered, "you are worried and upset about many things, but only one thing is needed. Mary has chosen what is better, and it will not be taken away from her" (Luke 10:40–42).

Martha was indeed completing an important task but sometimes we must give up even "important" things to spend time with Jesus not just offer Him the butt end of our day. The text says she was distracted. If she was distracted that would suggest that there was a more important task on which she needed to concentrate, or that she was trying to do too many things at once. In a similar situation we may tackle a task with bad grace. Then we don't complete the task well, or we create a bad atmosphere—or both! She was distracted, and in her distraction, she was going to distract others too. She was too busy serving Jesus to listen to Him. The cry of her heart was really: "Don't you care?" The tender repetition of her name shows that He did indeed care. And His advice gave her the solution. Pick the more important thing for you and everyone else.

Speaking as someone usually in the kitchen myself, I have a great deal of sympathy for Martha! The wonderful thing is that so too did Jesus. We are not told what Martha decided to do but I like to think that she sat and listened to Jesus, then everyone else pitched in to help make the meal at the end of the day.

If you genuinely think you don't have a spare minute (then you're too busy) but ask God to help you find creative ways to think of Him and His word during the day. Copy a Bible verse and carry it around with you. Look at it throughout the day and meditate on it when you have time. Daily readings may have a place, but you need to start cutting up and chewing your own food at some point. You cannot constantly rely on someone else to do this for you.

Read the story of Joseph or Moses or some other biblical person over a few days and then meditate upon the story. Ask yourself some questions about why they did the things they did, and said the things they said? What can you learn about God, and what can you learn about yourself, from these accounts? If you can read and have a Bible in your own language you are truly blessed. Some Christians over the ages would have given anything to have had that privilege. We should make full use of this blessing. Audio bibles are available and if you are tech savvy, I am sure you can think of other ways to make sure you have at least one square meal a day. Don't keep existing on milk. If you have no idea what I mean read this extract from Hebrews:

> We have much to say about this, but it is hard to explain because you are slow to learn. In fact, though by this time you ought to be teachers, you need someone to teach you the elementary truths of God's word all over again. You need milk, not solid food! Anyone who lives on milk, being still an infant, is not acquainted with the teaching about righteousness. But solid food is for the mature, who by constant use have trained themselves to distinguish good from evil (Heb 5:11–14). (See also 1 Cor 3:1–4).

Bible study will also help cut-off one of the other roots that a covetous spirit may take to try to rule your life: to deceive you with false teaching. The more familiar you are with the Bible and the voice of God which you hear there, the less likely you are to be fooled by a false one.

In addition, having a close friend or small group of Christian friends who you can openly share deep and personal issues with, is an excellent way to deal with any sin. Confessing and discussing with your husband or wife too may be helpful, depending upon the circumstances and the nature of the problem.

Count your Blessings

God loves an attitude of gratitude. Therefore, it is truly helpful to count your blessings.

Without much thought you could probably list fifty or more very quickly. Here are just a few things that I managed to type in one minute:

I am grateful that I am saved
Have a bible
Have the gift of sight
Have family
Friends
Have been taught to read
Had an education
Have a home
A bed to sleep in

Can walk
Can smell
Am not in pain
Live in a stable nation
Have access to medical care -
Especially a dentist
Painkillers are freely available
Have food in my fridge to cook a meal with tonight
Am warm
Have transport
Clothes
A computer
A radio
Earphones
The weather and seasons
Bird song

There are so many things for which we forget to be grateful. It is easy to focus on what we haven't got and forget all that we have. Count your blessings, count them one by one and it will surprise you what the Lord has done!

Consider the Motivation for your Covetousness

Whilst still searching for suggestions to help with covetousness it is worth looking again at the account of Achan in the book of Joshua. He took a beautiful cloak of Babylonian origin, gold, and silver. What was he hoping to do with the cloak? When was he ever going to be able to wear it? He had already buried it underground.

One aspect of covetousness which perhaps we could think about, and address is what do we really want the coveted item for? How are we going to use it? Do we need it? Achan stole the goods he saw and coveted but we may have similar temptations whilst shopping or looking at items online. Perhaps buying the item may put us into debt or further into debt. We should consider that before we head to the checkout, or press: confirm purchase. We all see things that we like and want, maybe right there and then is the time to stop, pause and consider our motivation. We need to practise saying "No" to our flesh. Sometimes, like Amnon, we can finish by hating the very thing we coveted or throw that new dress to the back of the wardrobe and never wear it. Pausing for a moment may be all we need to do before dashing headlong into trouble: "calmness can lay great errors to rest ..." (Eccl 10:4). Examining why we covet the things that we do may help in overcoming the covetous impulse.

Repent Quickly

Achan's sin of coveting the items that he discovered was not one that had been honed and refined over days or even years, he saw them and took them. Or did he? Surely the issue goes further back. His desire for the goods was obviously greater than his desire to obey God; even greater than a reverent fear of God, which we know is the beginning of all wisdom. This attitude had probably not developed overnight, but it was revealed in the incident of the stolen goods from Jericho. God says several times in His word that He desires obedience more than sacrifice. One of the ways we demonstrate our love for Him is by our obedience.

Finally, regarding Achan, was he without hope the minute he stole the items, or did he have time to repent? Imagine he had arrived home with his plunder and decided he had done an extremely foolish thing. Maybe a member of his family may have had a stern word with him and persuaded him on a different course of action other than hiding the items underground. They were under his tent, so it is difficult to believe that others close to him did not know they were there. With a repentant change of heart, he could have taken the items to Joshua and asked God for forgiveness. Some form of punishment may still have ensued, or it may not. We don't know.

Instead of which he endured an agonising countdown until the finger was firmly pointed at him and all chance for repentance was gone. He was found guilty. There are many lessons we can learn from this account of Achan and his covetous impulse.

Don't be an Enabler

Not only should you yourself not covet but you should not play a part in fulfilling someone else's covetous desires. You can be an enabler. When Ahab was told "No" by Naboth he had not really accepted that "No." He had used a tactic which is often used by people who want their own way but lack the competence, character, or pro-activeness to get it themselves—he sulked. He sulked and was angry. He knew Jezebel was a much more powerful character and could get him what he wanted, and she did. Hopefully, if we are enablers we would not consider going to the lengths of false accusations of wrong-doing and commissioning murder, but we may nevertheless enable a coveter to get their own way.

Consider a wife who sulks because she wants a bigger house, new car, new settee, new handbag, and her husband far from trying to make her see that this is nothing but covetousness (if indeed it is—she may need a new settee!) just gets it for her. Even if it means he must work longer hours and see less of the children. The situation can also be reversed. A husband may desire better golf clubs, new car, or the latest iPhone, instead of spending the money more sensibly. It is of course much more difficult when children are involved because often our judgment can be ignored. Everyone wants their children to have the best but even this can cross the line into covetousness. We should be teaching them better life lessons, not stoking a wrong attitude to possessions.

Do not Add or Subtract from the Word of God

The account of Eve in the Garden of Eden demonstrates that though her focus appeared to be the fruit it was not that alone that she coveted; it was something that the fruit could bestow:

> "When the woman saw that the fruit of the tree was good for food and pleasing to the eye, and also desirable for gaining wisdom, she took some and ate it. She also gave some to her husband, who was with her, and he ate it" (Gen 3:6).

Yes, the fruit looked good to eat but she really coveted the fact that it would give her wisdom and knowledge. Satan also suggested to her that she would be like God, knowing good and evil. It may be helpful to consider this factor with items that we covet. Do we desire a bigger house because we need a bigger house or is the purpose to impress acquaintances, friends, or relatives? As the saying goes: you work hard to buy things you don't really need, to impress people you don't really like. What a waste of your life's energy. A better use of your time may be to consider the reasons that you are coveting a particular thing and there you may find the real worm that has entered your apple. Once you understand the nature of the worm you may be better able to deal with it.

Eve also made the problem worse for herself by adding to God's word, something which at a cursory glance could be seen as quite insignificant:

"'You must not eat fruit from the tree that is in the middle of the garden, *and you must not touch it,* or you will die'" (Gen 3:3 emphasis mine). In Genesis 2:16 when God gives the command to Adam, He does not say "you must not touch it" He just says: "'you must not eat from the tree of knowledge.'" Obviously, it would be foolish to try to sail as close to the wind as you can, by touching a fruit that you cannot eat, but once having touched it and finding that there is no ill effect it may have encouraged Eve to go further. She had added to God's word ever so slightly and the consequences were dire. It may have been Adam that had made this addition, possibly hoping to emphasise the seriousness of the command. We have no account of God directly giving this command to Eve after all. Whichever one of them had added to His word, the consequence was the same.

The Pharisees did a similar thing putting "a hedge" around God's laws to prevent people from breaking them. The fourth commandment said that people should not work on the Sabbath. There were other places in the Torah too where it was made clear that other types of activity were forbidden and were a little more specific. Not content to leave it at that the rabbis went on to make their own definitions of what did, and did not, constitute work, and prohibited these activities also. Thinking of some of the encounters Jesus had with them in His lifetime, many were regarding conflicts raised by these additional rules. "'Then he said to them, "The Sabbath was made for man, not man for the Sabbath"'" (Mark 2:27). They too had added to the word of God to the detriment of all.

Practise Patience and Don't Live in a Fantasy World.

A further element that covetousness can exhibit is that of impatience. It is not necessarily that God is not going to give us what we covet but He is not going to give it to us now! As Adam and Eve had matured in their relationship with God, they may possibly have gained the wisdom and knowledge of which they were so desirous. Patience and self-control are virtues which we should covet because they will help us in the battle against covetousness!

These qualities are fruit of the spirit as mentioned in Galatians chapter 5. God is keen to help you grow this fruit and may have deliberately put you in a position where something you are legitimately desiring and know is part of His plan for you seems completely out of reach. He is possibly helping you to grow that element of patience which may be necessary to effectively wield whatever gift He has in mind for you, when He decides the time is right for you to exercise it. Many times in scripture, we are wisely told to wait on the Lord.

Nipping Lust in the Bud

We see that covetousness is also associated with lust and a desire that becomes so overwhelming that it can take over our lives. If lust and covetousness have mastered us, then they are now in control. We have become slaves to that passion. What can we do? We need to be vigilant and nip these things in the bud when they are easier to deal with. Paul talks about capturing every thought for Christ. We need to put this into practise. If we feel we are being taken over by some overwhelming desire, we need to pray and ask others to pray for us too. Guard your heart says the Bible.

If you do not deal with these unhealthy thoughts quickly, they will take root and you may begin to dwell on whatever you fantasise about coveting. The more you think about it, the more the desire will grow. The consequence may be that you will strenuously pursue the thing or person you are coveting, possibly breaking most of the ten commandments in the process. In addition, you may start to live in an imagined world instead of the real one, where you fantasise that you already possess the thing or person you covet and spend hours daydreaming about this make-believe world. Then much of your time and energy will be given to this diversion, distracting you from more healthy pursuits.

I once heard a conversation in which a man was telling a complete stranger what he would do if he won the lottery. His plan was so detailed and expansive that it was obvious he had given a lot of thought and mental energy to this event that was never going to happen. So real was this world that he could describe it in great detail to a total stranger. I am not here decrying the necessity of planning or having aspirations or even just the occasional daydream. I am talking about a long-term, in depth, fantasy life, that is never going to materialise, and its only function is to make you unhappy in your real life by drawing you further into its clutches. You only have a limited amount of energy and time. This life is quite short. Don't waste it trying to obtain things that are not good for you or those around you and are counter to God's good plan for your life. Try to enjoy and inhabit today as it is:

"This is the day the Lord has made; let us rejoice and be glad in it" (Ps 118:24)

4

Any Good Things about Covetousness?

A Beautiful Tree—Being the Individual God Intended

> Now, you that have lately been converted, do not go and learn all the pretty phrases that we are accustomed to use. Do not go and sit down at the feet of your dear teacher in the class and feel that you must talk just like him. Strike out your own course. Be yourself. "But I should be odd," say you. All right: so is your pastor. You need not mind that. You will not be the only odd body about. Be encouraged by that. I think that a little of what people call oddness is just, after all, leaving God's work alone. All the trees that God makes are odd. The Dutchmen clip them round or make them into peacocks, but that style of gardening is not to our mind. And some people say, "What a lovely tree!" I say, "What a horribly ugly thing it is." Why not let the tree grow as God would have it? Do not clip yourselves round or square but keep your freshness. There will be no two Christian men exactly alike if they do that.[1]

As Charles Spurgeon points out here, God wants us to be individuals—albeit individuals that belong to a body. Therefore, not everything in this book will necessarily apply to you. It is appropriate to state this here because this section is about desires. The desires of our heart and the desires that God has for us and has given to us. You are an individual just as

---

1. Spurgeon, Charles. Sermon on: "*Freshness*" para 9

God intended you to be. Follow the godly desires He has given you and you will grow into the beautiful tree that He planned you would be from the beginning of time. Albeit a tree that may look a little odd to others but to God you will be beautiful.

Coveting a Relationship with God

In all the definitions we have looked at we can see that the root meaning of 'to covet' is to desire strongly. As a result of the Fall all our emotions and desires have been twisted and contorted from their original form. Coveting is really a legitimate desire gone wrong.

There are three major ways that this has happened that we have examined so far.

Firstly, it is lusting after a greater number of temporal things that go beyond what God has determined is eternally best for you. Secondly, it can also be about timing; not being patient. The Lord may have given you a godly desire, but you must wait upon His timing for that desire to come to fruition. Thirdly, it can also be wanting what belongs to someone else.

An extreme shorthand way of expressing this drive may be: 'I want it!' You could add to this: even if it belongs to someone else or even if I could possibly have it legitimately if I were patient. It is idolatry.

However, are there some things that we should legitimately earnestly desire or covet?

Looking at the first of these issues which is: wanting more things than God has determined is eternally best for us, we can return to "The Parable of The Rich Fool." (Luke 12:13–21). This exposition of Jesus began with a question concerning inheritance and one brother feeling he was not being treated fairly by another brother in that regard. The parable concludes with this piece of advice: "'This is how it will be with anyone who stores up things for himself but is not rich towards God'" (Luke 12:21). What is being condemned is the desire to amass lots of goods for yourself: covetousness, and the advice to counter it is to be "rich towards God." Instead of desiring lots of possessions we should channel that desire towards God and the things of His kingdom.

We can be rich in many ways. It can be money or goods, or even referring to a good source or supply of something. For example: water, friends, talents, land, or in the case of the farmer in the parable, rich in crops. We can have access to an unending source of riches in God but not necessarily things that the world would consider riches. The source is there, we just need to tap into it, but even before that we need to desire it.

Think about how you pursue things that you desire in other areas of your life? What about someone you desire to get to know? How do you try to accomplish that? How much time do you spend thinking about them; contacting them; taking an interest in their interests; just getting to know them. Do you feel that way about God? We are supposed to love God first and foremost, above all else and above anyone else.

How would that look in practise? It would look like Jesus. He is the only one that has ever lived that has been totally sold out for God throughout His life. He was rich towards God, but He also wanted to share the riches: share His wisdom; teaching; revelations from the Father, and gifts. He coveted/desired God and that was fine.

One relationship in life it is beneficial and legitimate to desire strongly, is a relationship with God. You cannot go beyond what He has designated as eternally best for you in this area. Neither does He belong exclusively to someone else, so in this relationship you can covet away to your heart's content.

It is noticeable how many cults make it hard to gain access to the main guru or god that they worship. There is often many levels and initiations that you must complete before you are considered worthy to enter their presence and even then, access is limited, curtailed, and infrequent. We like the idea of exclusivity; something to which only a select few have access. Sometimes the harder it is the more we are drawn to it. It probably plays to the pride that makes us want to earn our salvation. God, on the other hand is available all the time, everywhere. As we have already said, each one of us will have a unique relationship with Him to some extent because we are unique individuals, and how deep and habitual that relationship can be will depend on how much time, energy, and desire we give to it. You may feel you have little time but if you have the desire, God will do the rest, though it may not be as quickly as you would like. Remember His providential care and attention to detail.

We can covet a relationship with God.

Coveting Spiritual Gifts

As well as "coveting" God it is good to earnestly desire spiritual gifts. This is something that Paul emphasises in his letter to the Corinthians. "But covet earnestly the best gifts: and yet shew I unto you a more excellent way" (1 Cor 12:31 KJV).

As I mentioned at the beginning of the book it can be hard to untangle these three "sisters" which we are studying. There is much cross-over between all three emotions not to mention confusion arising from the words used to describe them. The King James Bible is the only translation that interprets this word as covet the others usually preferring "earnestly desire." The Greek word used is *zeloo* from which we get our word zealous or jealous, so it could easily slot into the section on jealousy but in this book, it is more appropriately situated here.

This verse comes at the end of a passage when Paul has been considering that we are one body made up of many parts, then listing some of the gifts the body needs to operate efficiently.

> Now you are the body of Christ and each one of you is part of it. And in the church God has appointed first of all apostles, second prophets, third teachers, then workers of miracles, also those having gifts of healing, those able to help others, those with gifts of administration and those speaking in different kinds of tongues. Are all apostles? Are all prophets? Are all teachers? Do all work miracles? Do all have gifts of healing? Do all speak with tongues? Do all interpret?'
> But eagerly desire the greater gifts (1 Cor 12:27–31).

We are to eagerly desire these gifts. They are for the building up and functioning of the body of Christ. Therefore, they are not something which we are coveting or earnestly desiring for our own aggrandisement or advantage. They are a gift to the body of Christ. We are merely a conduit through which Christ is ministering that specific gift at a particular time. We need to keep this in mind otherwise we can fall prey to pride.

We should earnestly desire spiritual gifts not spiritual positions: some ministry position in the church which we have our eye on that is already filled by someone else. If you feel you are called to some specific role you could always offer to assist the person already discharging it. Certain gifts mean that some Christians can seem more high profile than others. Conversely some gifts can seem very mundane or insignificant. Almost as important as not trying to oust someone from a position to make way for elevating yourself, is not to despise the gift you yourself have been given. Do not: "despise the day of small things" (Zech 4:10).

Just be the best you can be at whatever you have been tasked to do and God will take care of the rest. He knows you better than anyone and He can easily raise people up or, take them down!

Earnestly Desiring God's Laws and Statutes

In addition to spiritual gifts, we are also to earnestly desire/covet *(chamad)* God's laws and statutes more than gold. We find this advice in Psalm 19:10: "More to be desired are they than gold, yea, than much fine gold; sweeter also than honey and the honeycomb" (KJV).

I don't think many people could be said to love following laws, statutes, and commands. Perhaps if we look at this conundrum the other way round, we may have more insight and therefore ask ourselves the question: why do people covet gold? Though we may want to wear it as jewellery usually it is what gold can offer us that we really covet. It promises protection, safety, a life of ease and freedom, a life free from restrictions of daily work. Time to do what we want. It offers power, popularity, fame.

There is a person in the Bible who had all these things and added to all these blessings, he was given wisdom too. That is of course King Solomon. He really was the man with everything. Yet, as well as writing Proverbs, he is also credited with writing the book of Ecclesiastes. This is how it begins:

> "The words of the Teacher, a son of David, king in Jerusalem: "Meaningless! Meaningless!" says the Teacher. "Utterly meaningless! Everything is meaningless." What does man gain from all his labours at which he toils under the sun? (Eccl 1:1–3)

There is not time here to go through all the many and various experiences that he had tried and the things that he had acquired that he now considers meaningless. A few he mentions are: study, wisdom, and knowledge; many acquisitions of precious metals; pleasure and sensual delights of various types; gardens and building projects; many slaves; exotic, eclectic, articles and animals; a harem. In fact, he says: "I denied myself nothing my eye desired; I refused my heart no pleasure" (Eccl: 2:10). Doesn't that sound like covetousness?

Yet reading the book of Ecclesiastes he does not appear to be a happy, satisfied, man. Instead, he sounds like an old man full of regrets who has had his fill of every possible thing and is weary of it all. A world-weary soul. It would very much seem as if he were suffering from acedia, which is weariness in spiritual things as well as things of this world.

This can all appear very counter-intuitive and paradoxical because I am stating that Solomon who was the wisest person who ever lived and knew God's laws and statutes better than anyone of his age, finished like this! Yet, I am also saying that according to Psalm 19 if you covet God's laws above all else, you will find them sweeter than honey and that "in keeping them is great reward" (Ps 19:11).

Solomon was not only given wisdom, but he would have had access to the Law. Jesus often referred to the Law. This denotes the first five books of the Bible: Genesis, Exodus, Leviticus, Numbers and Deuteronomy. It contains all that the psalm is referring to variously in verses 7–9 as: law, statutes, precepts, commands, and ordinances. In addition to that, as a King, who was following the law, Solomon should have known and completed the following: "When he takes the throne of his kingdom, he is to write for himself on a scroll a copy of this law, taken from that of the priests, who are Levites" (Deut 17:18).

The problem seems to be not that he did not know the Law but rather that he didn't keep it.

He wrote or collected Proverbs that warned about many things, including adultery. Yet he had seven hundred wives and three hundred concubines according to 1 Kings 11:3 The law also contains commands not to marry foreign wives. This prohibition was because the wives may lead the husband into idolatry. This is exactly what happened to Solomon:

> King Solomon however, loved many foreign women besides Pharaoh's daughter—Moabites, Ammonites, Edomites, Sidonians and Hittites. They were from nations about which the Lord had told the Israelites: "You must not intermarry with them, because they will surely turn your hearts after their gods." Nevertheless, Solomon held fast to them in love. He had seven hundred wives of royal birth and three hundred concubines and his wives led him astray (1 Kgs 11:1–3).

The issue was not that Solomon did not know the commandments of God, but he did not love them or follow them. His heart was lured away to covet other things. As we have already seen, coveting can lead to breaking most of the other ten commandments, and this seems to be the case for Solomon.

The constant refrain of Ecclesiastes is: "under the sun." "'I have seen all things that are done under the sun; all of them are meaningless, a chasing after the wind'" (Eccl 1:14). Disobedience and idolatry led Solomon to focusing on this material, earthly, life—the things under the sun. God is not under the Sun. God is not under anything. God created the Sun. Solomon had lost sight of all this wonder of life because he had lost sight of his first love, his love of God. He does seem to have realised this in extremis. At the end of Ecclesiastes, he says:

"Now all has been heard; here is the conclusion of the matter:

Fear God and keep his commandments, for this is the whole duty of man" (Eccl 12:13).

But is seems to be said with a spirit of sadness and resignation. The words of someone who has wasted a huge percentage of their life on worthless things. On things "under the sun." On the one hand we are presented with the life of someone who has coveted the pleasures of this world and been led into the arms of Mammon. On the other we are told in Psalm 19 that if we covet the law of God: it revives the soul; makes wise the simple; gives joy to the heart and light to the eyes. We are also assured that His law will endure for ever and is altogether righteous. His laws are more precious than pure gold and sweeter than honey—than honey from the comb. Direct from its source, unadulterated and pure. We can have life in abundance, if we covet the laws of God and love them and Him. But we also need to obey them too.

We can legitimately desire or covet a relationship with God our Father and the spiritual gifts He has for us, when we are mature enough to handle them safely and the time is right. A sign of our maturity and rightly applied desire is that we love His laws and obey them.

5

Jealousy: Joseph and his Brothers

It's Mine!

All the three sisters have in common the fact of desiring something or someone. Jealousy mainly differs from covetousness and envy in that often there is a sense of loss that accompanies it. This may be an actual loss; fear of a potential loss; or even a perceived loss. I may covet someone else's husband, but I would be jealous if someone stole mine, because rightfully, he should be committed to me and "belong" to me. The crossover between the different faces of these emotions is sometimes hard to untangle as they have many similarities and one can change into another over time and become a two-headed or even three-headed monster. The English definition for jealousy is to be distrustful of the faithfulness of a partner; feeling or showing resentment of someone for their achievements, possessions, or perceived advantages; fiercely protective of one's rights or possessions.

The origin of the word dates to the 12th century and is originally from the old French and usually meant: keen, avaricious, or jealous. This was in turn from the Latin *zelous* or zeal which sometimes meant jealousy, as we would understand it now, but was more often used in the good sense of emulation, rivalry, zeal. The Greek *zeloo* was an onomatopoeic word (imitating the sound of boiling water; to bubble over because of heat) hence to burn with zeal. Expressing the meaning of being deeply committed to someone or something; to set your heart completely upon. From *zelos* zeal, translated as jealousy, fury, or eagerness.

These are all describing a hot, fierce, emotion.

A Dysfunctional Family

We will examine some ways this emotion is represented in a very familiar Bible story.

The accounts of Jacob and his family are so riven with issues of jealousy that it is difficult to pick one or two out of so many. Jealousy just seemed to be part of their family's make-up and indeed this can be the same with families today. This is possibly what the Bible means when it talks about the sins of the fathers being visited upon their children. It is not that God places these sins on the children's heads but rather a family dynamic is being perpetuated. Of course, individuals can step out of this with God's help, and sometimes without it too.

In the family of Jacob, the presence of jealousy can be traced back to several incidents which are interconnected. Jacob coveted his elder brother's birth-right so much that he connived with his mother to try to seize this. When the deception was discovered the fury of his brother meant he had to leave his family home and go to the dwelling of his uncle Laban who lived miles away. Here he met his match. Laban was also very good at conniving to get his own way and tricked Jacob into marrying his elder daughter, Leah. Jacob only wanted to marry the younger daughter Rachel, whom he really loved. This manoeuvre by Laban resulted in both his daughters being married to the same man at the same time.

Leah knew Jacob loved Rachel and not her, so the grounds for jealousy to thrive in this situation were very rich. Not to mention the fact that they were now all tied together in an intimate way for life! Rachel had great difficulty in conceiving whereas Leah had many children, so jealousy was stoked between the sisters in yet another way. Eventually, when Rachel finally had children, they were the apple of their Father's eye, and he made this obvious. More logs were thrown onto the fire of jealousy that was already well stoked and raging. It was all going to blow up and boil over at some point, and it did.

The Pot Boils Over

Joseph, Rachel's eldest son was not only his father's favourite alongside his full-brother Benjamin, but it seemed he was God's favourite too. He had been blessed with great gifts, one of which was the ability to interpret dreams. However, as we mentioned earlier character development needs to work alongside, or even come before, spiritual gifts. If this is not the case then the gift can be used wrongly, insensitively, or in ways that countermand its effective use.

Joseph's character would need many years of work. He had hard and difficult lessons to learn before he became highly skilled at using his gifts. The dreams that he had and told his family about can be found in Genesis 37:1–10. He accurately interpreted these dreams; that his brothers and his Mum and Dad would bow down before him, but it was going to be many, tough, years before this became a reality. (His real mother Rachel had been dead for some time when the incident came to pass, but possibly Leah or Bilhah had stepped into this role and are being referred to here.)

It is after this incident of relating his dreams to his family that we read: "His brothers were jealous of him, but his father kept the matter in mind" (Gen 37:11). There are a few things that we can notice already. The father, Jacob, was responsible for stoking this jealousy. He was foolish to have made this so obvious in so many ways, for example by buying Joseph a special coat. "Let us not become conceited, provoking and envying each other" (Gal 5:26).

It is extremely unkind to provoke jealousy. If someone had a broken arm, hopefully you would not deliberately hit them on it. Many people have sore emotional spots and if we are aware of them, we should not try to exacerbate their hurt and inflame it. For example, if you knew someone had just had a miscarriage or stillbirth it would be very insensitive to start showing them pictures of your own happy, smiling, baby. If you were doing it deliberately that would be cruel. Or if you know someone had a poor relationship with their father or an absent father, to boast about how much your father does for you and loves you would be mean-spirited.

Obviously, we all have sore spots and sometimes we are unintentionally insensitive or just unaware of the hurts of others, but if we know and deliberately choose to inflame the wound, then that is sinful.

> Now Israel loved Joseph more than any other of his sons, because he had been born to him in his old age; and he made a richly ornamented robe for him. When his brothers saw that their father loved him more than any of them, they hated him and could not speak a kind word to him (Gen 37:3–4).

Jealousy: Joseph and his Brothers

Very often in scripture we see that the punishment inflicted says something about the sin that has been committed. In other words, the punishment fits the crime. I think this is to make us reflect and repent. Jacob inflamed his other sons' jealousy of Joseph whether he meant to or not and the result was he lost that beloved son for twenty years. Joseph was taken away from him.

Do not deliberately provoke jealousy it is not only very unkind but also potentially dangerous.

Admittedly Joseph bore some of the blame. He was very tactless in the way he shared his dreams, but he was young and immature. In addition, he gave a bad report to his father about how his brothers were performing their job. "Joseph, a young man of seventeen, was tending the flocks with his brothers, the sons of Bilhah and the sons of Zilpah, his father's wives, and he brought their father a bad report about them" (Gen 37:2). You can see the fuel being poured upon the already raging fire. This is not to excuse the jealousy of the brothers because in many ways it was a family affair! Jacob shares some responsibility and, in a minor way, Joseph too.

Jealousy usually has some element of loss associated with it, yet what loss had the brothers suffered? If anything, Joseph was the one who had suffered loss. His mother had died when his brother Benjamin was born. This may have contributed to Jacob spoiling Joseph. He may have been trying to make up for the loss of a mother. We could say that as brothers they all felt entitled to the same love from their father. This was not the reality in which they lived, and they probably did feel this favouritism as a type of loss. In addition, they had suffered years of seeing their mother Leah, being treated less favourably. Jacob was her husband too. She was entitled to his love. Proverbs tells us:

> Under three things the earth trembles; under four it cannot bear up: a servant who becomes a king, a fool who is full of food; an unloved woman who is married; and a maidservant who displaces her mistress (Prov 30:21–23).

An unloved wife makes the earth tremble. "When the Lord saw that Leah was not loved, he opened her womb; but Rachel was barren". (Gen 29:3).

The Hebrew word 'sane', here translated as unloved can also carry the meaning of enmity, hatred, turned against, as well as, unloved. All of which seem to suggest the situation could have been worse than we may have imagined. It is easy to see why Jacob felt this way about Leah. He had been tricked into marrying her when he only ever wanted Rachel.

Leah may well have been deceived also. Some rabbis believe that neither she nor Rachel knew anything concerning the wedding arrangements and that her father had handled everything. Possibly she was complicit in the deception but either way she was unloved, possibly hated. Not only was she unloved, but her sister was greatly loved by *her husband*. She witnessed this day after day, year after year. Her children witnessed it too. She felt the legitimate loss of the love of her husband. Perhaps the incident of the mandrakes helps elucidate this:

> During wheat harvest, Reuben went into the fields and found some mandrake plants which he brought to his mother Leah. Rachel said to Leah, "Please give me some of your son's mandrakes." But she said to her, "Wasn't it enough that you took away my husband? Would you take away my son's mandrakes too?"
>
> "Very well" Rachel said, "he can sleep with you tonight in return for your son's mandrakes."
>
> So when Jacob came in from the fields that evening, Leah went out to meet him.
>
> "You must sleep with me," she said. "I have hired you with my son's mandrakes."
>
> So he slept with her that night. God listened to Leah, and she became pregnant and bore Jacob a fifth son (Gen 30:14–17).

Here Leah says to her sister: "Wasn't it enough that you took away my husband?" We can see and hear her hurt but in addition Reuben, her eldest son, obviously felt his mother's pain too. He, along with the rest of his brothers had seen her rejection and sadness. The whole situation is soaked with hurt and jealousy.

Even most people who are generally biblically illiterate, know the outcome of this story. Eventually the brothers have had enough and decide to get rid of the hated Joseph. He had become the focal point for all this accumulated jealousy. Initially they were going to kill him, but Reuben wanted to save his life (Gen 37:12–36) and played for time by having Joseph put into a water cistern. It is unclear where Reuben goes but he is not there when a caravan of Ishmaelites passes by. Judah proposes a different plan, to sell Joseph into slavery and in the absence of Reuben, the rest agree. So begins years of slavery for Joseph, years of guilt for the brothers, and years of sorrow for their father, Jacob. Jealousy. Jealousy the cause of so much

Jealousy: Joseph and his Brothers

pain. Jealousy provoked, jealousy fed, and jealousy unchecked. A monster fed on pain and loss; resulted in pain and loss. It's very, very, sad.

But God . . .

The spotlight in the Bible then turns to Joseph and how God uses this situation to develop his character to complement the amazing gifts that he had already been given. The climax of the story is the famous statement made to his brothers years later: "'You intended to harm me, but God intended it for good to accomplish what is now being done, the saving of many lives'" (Gen 50:20). We can see expressed in this verse the growth of Joseph's spiritual maturity. He had come to see the situation through God's eyes rather than his own which means he could let go of any inclination he had for revenge and let forgiveness and mercy reign supreme.

However, the spotlight for the purposes of this book is not really on Joseph in Egypt but rather looking back to the jealous brothers in Canaan to see how they are progressing. What spiritual maturity have they gained now that the object and focus of their jealousy has been removed? Is this the end of jealousy? Is the jealous spirit that had ruled their lives for so long now lying down defeated never to raise her head again? It would appear not.

Jealousy remains and has now been joined by other equally horrible emotions; guilt of a sin committed and unable to be confessed; fear of discovery; and sorrow for their grieving father—as well as probably great irritation with him too. Far from getting rid of Joseph they had merely made him more present. Of Jacob we are told: "All his sons and daughters came to comfort him, but he refused to be comforted. "No," he said, "in mourning will I go down to the grave to my son." So his father wept for him" (Gen 37:35). Sometimes a dead person can be just as annoying as a living one, with the added element that they can be made to seem more noble in death than they ever were in life.

Many years later when they are contemplating a second journey to Egypt and needed to take Benjamin, we read this: "But Jacob said "My son will not go down there with you; his brother is dead and he is the only one left. If harm comes to him on the journey you are taking, you will bring my grey head down to the grave in sorrow'" (Gen 42:38).

"The only one left"?! Nine of his other sons were stood before him. I wonder how that felt? It is possible and probably that he merely meant the only one of Rachel's sons left, but even that tells a tale and itself betrays a mindset. From the brothers' perspective it does not seem that the supposedly dead Joseph was proving any easier to live with than the live one had been, and now Jacob seems fixated on Benjamin. I am sure the brothers were on their own emotional journey, and we know that they were still plagued with guilt about their treatment of Joseph because over twenty years later:

> They said to one another, "Surely we are being punished because of our brother. We saw how distressed he was when he pleaded with us for his life, but we would not listen; that's why this distress has come upon us." Reuben replied, "Didn't I tell you not to sin against the boy? But you wouldn't listen! Now we must give an accounting for his blood" (Gen 42:21–22).

6

Judah

Breaking Free

During the interim period prior to the trips to Egypt, the only brother about whom we have much information is Judah. His tale provides a strange interlude in the biblical story of Joseph. The account of this can be found in Genesis chapter 38.

How was Judah trying to cope with the aftermath of selling his own brother into slavery? The first thing that we read about him is this: "At that time, Judah left his brothers and went down to stay with a man of Adullam named Hirah" (Gen 38:1).

Probably the family of Jacob, had by necessity, lived quite an isolated life, albeit within the sphere of a very large family. We know that back in Paddan Aram they had needed to separate themselves from their neighbours and relatives, Uncle Laban proving to be quite hostile. Once back in Canaan the debacle with the inhabitants of Shechem had ensued because of the incident involving their sister Dinah, and the tribe had to move from that area too. This may have made them cautious about getting too close to other tribes in the area who in turn, having heard of their behaviour at Shechem were equally cautious about them. In fact, that was a concern of Jacob at the time: "Then Jacob said to Simeon and Levi, "You have brought trouble on me by making me a stench to the Canaanites and Perizzites, the people living in this land. We are few in number, and if they join forces against me and attack me, I and my household will be destroyed."' (Gen 34:30). For various reasons the household of Jacob had for years been quite an incestuous and inward-looking group. Incestuous in the broader sense of very close and resistant to outside influence.

Judah decides to break free from this and set out on his own. He moves to Adullam. Sometimes to conquer an issue we need to move away from the seat of the problem. Whilst we remain, torturing ourselves, it will not heal. It does not mean to say that we cannot later return when the situation, or we ourselves, have changed, and of course all situations are different. It is interesting though how often God takes someone He wants to use right out of their current situation. Abraham had to move from his familiar surroundings in Ur. Jacob had to escape from Esau and flee to Paddam Aram. Joseph is forcibly taken to Egypt. Moses is exiled from Egypt for forty years, and here we see Judah too moves away. As Joseph was changing and maturing in Egypt so Judah was going through his own metamorphosis in Adullam. A family or tribe or even people of a particular city or district may have their own way of seeing things. A modern term would be groupthink. We need to escape this to enable us to see things differently, with a clarity gained from distance and exile. Moving away was heading in a different direction both physically, mentally, and spiritually. It is possibly the beginnings of repentance. Judah, for whatever reason, broke away.

The Good Friend

The second thing that we could deduce from this passage is that he had a particularly close friend, Hirah. This friend was close enough to accompany him on journeys and be party to very personal and sensitive negotiations that he needed to make regarding his encounter with Tamar. Initially Hirah is referred to as "a man of Adullam." He is mentioned twice more in this short chapter and on both occasions is called friend. He was no longer merely a man of Adullam, he is a friend.

Oh, the blessings of a good friend! Someone who Judah could talk to on the long journeys he had to make. Someone to share past and present issues with. Someone who liked him and cared about him and wanted what was best for him. Our society now makes much of professional counselling services and they may certainly have a place. However, all that troubled people often need is to be able to talk about an issue and examine it with someone who has their best interests at heart. A listening ear which will enable them to bring some of their problems and fears out into the open.

To see them for what they are and learn how to handle them. If they are a godly friend who can offer godly counsel, all the better.

Judah had eleven brothers or half-brothers but sometimes a friend is closer and to be valued and treasured even more. You have no choice about the family into which you were born, thankfully you can choose your friends. A friend chooses you too! Even just the love of a friend can be quite healing and very encouraging. They often see things in you which your family do not. Familiarity often blinds family members to your potential qualities and does not always provide a space for those qualities to flourish and mature.

Sometimes you may need space to grow and be able to see yourself differently; to be free of family expectations and infections. Certainly, it is not always necessary for everyone to have to break free of a family or cut ties with then. Often it is close family relationships that God uses to change us. You need to be sensitive to whatever the spirit is telling you personally to do.

Perseverance in Righteousness

We have looked at two issues that may have helped change Judah: moving away from his family and the cooking pot of jealousy that had thrived there; and acquiring a good friend. However, these are by no means the main events of this chapter.

Judah gets married and has three sons: Er, Onan and Shelah. In due course Er is married to Tamar. The Bible does not give detailed information as to the reasons for what happens next, but we are told: "Er, Judah's firstborn, was wicked in the Lord's sight; so the Lord put him to death" (Gen 38:7). Whilst we are given no details about Er's sins we are told why the second son is executed. He has failed to carry out his duty to father children on behalf of his brother.

> Then Judah said to Onan, "Lie with your brother's wife and fulfil your duty to her as a brother-in-law to produce offspring for your brother." But Onan knew that the offspring would not be his; so whenever he lay with his brother's wife, he spilled his semen on the ground to keep from producing offspring for his brother. What he did was wicked in the Lord's sight; so he put him to death also (Gen 38:8–10).

Judah who does not know the reasons for his sons' deaths believes that Tamar is the problem. He has one more son who she could marry but he sends her back to her own father's house to wait until Shelah, his next son, is old enough to carry out his duty on behalf of his dead brothers, or at least that's what he tells Tamar. "Judah then said to his daughter-in-law Tamar, "Live as a widow in your father's house until my son Shelah grows up." For he thought, "He may die too, just like his brothers." So Tamar went to live in her father's house" (Gen 38:11).

As we can see Judah had no intention of carrying on with this policy and sentencing another son to death and to be honest, who can blame him! Whatever we think of this custom and law it was obviously considered the righteous behaviour of the time and later codified by Moses:

> If brothers are living together and one of them dies without a son, his widow must not marry outside the family. Her husband's brother shall take her and marry her and fulfil the duty of a brother-in-law to her. The first son she bears shall carry on the name of the dead brother so that his name will not be blotted out from Israel (Deut 25: 5–6).

This was something that Henry VIII drew upon when he wanted to marry his brother Arthur's widow, Catherine of Aragon. After twenty years of marriage when he was lusting after (coveting) another woman, Anne Boleyn, he then felt that this verse was now the pertinent one: "If a man marries his brother's wife, it is an act of impurity; he has dishonoured his brother. They will be childless" (Lev 20:21).

It was much more complicated than the very brief description of the situation that has been given here, suffice to say it is important that we consult God with an aim of discovering what is His best will for our lives and the Bible will play a vital part in discovering what that may be. However, to come to the Bible searching for a verse which will help confirm what you have already decided you want to do is not seeking God on a situation. That is eisegesis not exegesis.

We are either diligently seeking God's will or we are merely seeking to have our will endorsed. It is possible to find a Bible verse which would suit most positions you would want to take in any given situation. With some creative redaction you can even find part of a verse that declares there is no God: "The fool says in his heart, "There is no God"" (Ps 14:1). Individual verses can be used and abused by all. As the apostle Paul explains in the book of Acts, we need the whole counsel of God to assist our deliberations as well as the help of the Holy Spirit to guide us to make godly decisions.

In the situation we are examining here Judah first does the right thing according to God, then he does the wrong thing. He recognises this after the incident with Tamar, when he discovered she was pregnant and that he was the father: "'She is more righteous than I, since I wouldn't give her to my son Shelah.'" (Gen 38:26)

Why is this relevant?

In the situation with Joseph, he was the one who suggested selling him into slavery. He did the wrong thing. Over twenty years later, Joseph's brother, Benjamin, is at risk of the same fate. Judah offers to redeem him. When given the second chance he does the right thing. He has truly repented. Not only had he truly repented but he proved it in the best way possible by not repeating a sin when placed in a very similar situation. He was not going to let another brother become a slave and was prepared to offer himself in exchange (Gen 44:17–34). In the incident with Tamar, he had initially done the right thing, but he hadn't persevered in righteousness, which we know is very important. He had probably also learned if you don't do the right thing God will still find a way to make sure it happens, and you may be the tool He uses to bring this about. He had been given lessons in both perseverance and righteousness as well as the omnipotence of God.

Even though Judah had sinned in his treatment of Tamar, God could still weave this episode into the fabric of His plan of salvation. Consider what would have been the situation without the incident regarding Tamar and Judah. If the tribe of Judah had not continued there would have been no King David, no Isaiah, hardly any of the minor prophets and no parents for the Messiah.

When considering the issue of jealousy, I am not entirely sure that if we had some scale on which to measure it, that Judah would have been anywhere near the top, when compared to the other brothers. However, Genesis 37:11 includes all the brothers when it says they were jealous of Joseph. Nevertheless, just as this interlude was refining Joseph's character to exercise his gifts well and with godly purpose, so too it was refining Judah.

Character of a Leader

He obviously had great leadership qualities that were nascent and needed to be honed. He appears to be pragmatic, decisive, persuasive, and even though he may have had some issues with jealousy, he does not appear to have allowed his emotions to entirely control his judgement, even at the young age when we first encounter him. He is not the oldest brother but the fourth in line. Yet in nearly all crisis situations in these chapters of Genesis he is taking the lead. It is he who suggests selling Joseph into slavery (Gen 37: 26–27). This is opportunistic, shows quick thinking and is extremely practical. They don't have to kill Joseph, his blood is not on their hands, yet he is removed.

Reuben, who was the oldest, and one who we would think of as the potential leader of the clan, had procrastinated, and had a vague idea of trying to rescue Joseph. However, he does not attempt to persuade his brothers or seem to have the character or charisma to carry the argument.

In addition, his plan was wholly impractical and far from resolving anything would have merely made the situation worse. Joseph now knew the full extent of the brother's animosity. They had discussed killing him and thrown him in a pit. He also had a track record of giving a bad report of his brothers to Jacob. How could Reuben possibly have expected to return him back to the family home and carry on as if nothing had happened? This is not to say that Judah did the right thing morally, far from it. But looking at the situation dispassionately his was a good, practical, solution.

Prior to the second journey to Egypt once again it is Judah who is decisive and helps overcome the objections of Jacob and allay his fears about Benjamin as best he can, as this has been the main obstacle to overcome in preparing for this second trip.

> Then Judah said to Israel his father, "Send the boy along with me and we will go at once, so that we and you and our children may live and not die. I myself will guarantee his safety; you can hold me personally responsible for him. If I do not bring him back to you and set him here before you, I will bear the blame before you all my life. As it is, if we had not delayed, we could have gone and returned twice"(Gen 43:8–10).

Again, Reuben had earlier offered a totally impractical solution: "Then Reuben said to his father, "You may put both of my sons to death if I do not bring him back to you. Entrust him to my care, and I will bring him back"" (Gen 42:37). Superficially this may seem a much bolder and costlier guarantee but in practise would never have been carried out, which everyone must have known. What incentive did Reuben really have to protect

Benjamin when he was really risking nothing? Judah's offer by contrast was bold and potentially costly and, once again, his argument carried the day.

Ultimately, we see that Judah had integrity. He meant what he said and was prepared to go through with his part of the contract. Something about his demeanour and manner had conveyed this conviction and confidence. The characteristics of a great leader. Finally, when all the tribe move to Egypt it is Judah who Jacob sends ahead to get directions. Symbolically, taking on the role of representative of the tribe; an ambassador.

Walking in Another Man's Shoes

Considering Judah and his road to repentance we see that God had put him in another man's shoes. The shoes of his father, Jacob. It is easy to overlook in all this that Judah had lost not one son but two. He now knew the pain of this first hand. The Bible does say that we reap what we sow and, as already mentioned, usually the punishment for sin is sometimes connected to the nature of the sin committed. However, we also see that on his road to repentance, Judah is blessed with two more sons. This is not to suggest that the original sons were replaced in his affections. I am sure he would always feel the mark of their loss, but it was a type of redemption for him and knowing the pain of the loss of two sons he was not willing to let that be inflicted on someone else, let alone his own father.

Possibly Judah had learned other things from his family situation too that he was unwilling to pass on. He did not have other wives and even after his wife died it seems he did not remarry. The sexual encounter with Tamar, who he had not recognised and believed to be a prostitute, was not repeated: "And he did not sleep with her again" (Gen 38:26). It may be stretching the little information that we have quite far, but it appears he did not want a repetition of the multiple wives and half-brother's scenario in which he had grown up.

Recovery, Change and Growth

From this account of Judah, we see several things that have helped him to escape from the toxic, family situation where jealousy had thrived, finally resulting in selling a brother into slavery. He had moved away because the family dynamic was in danger of warping and ruining his character. Instead of remaining to be at the mercy of forces beyond his control, he took charge of his own life. We can of course see God working behind the scenes and no doubt was instrumental in Judah's choices. He had begun his own family. He had at least one close friend in whom he confided. Additionally, just as Joseph's skills were maturing and developing in Egypt, so too were Judah's character and leadership qualities developing in his own form of exile.

Sometimes we may need to distance ourselves from a situation where jealousy is fuelled and thrives. Sometimes it is impossible for us to do so.

7

Jealousy: Leah and Rachel

An Unloved Wife

In the previous chapter we looked in some detail at the story of Judah and have already seen the deep emotional traps and entanglements by which his family were surrounded. Judah moved away from this environment. He could do this, but Rachel and Leah were tied to their situation for life. They could not divorce Jacob and set up home on their own as many are able to do in our society today. Neither could they go back home to their father, which may have been the only option available to them in that culture and era. It would initially seem that this situation would have been much harder for Leah, she was after all the third wheel, the unwanted, unloved, wife. However, God saw this and had pity on her: "When the Lord saw that Leah was not loved, he opened her womb, but Rachel was barren" (Gen 29:31).

Often in the Bible we have very little information with which to work when trying to find out more about some of its main characters. Here in Genesis, we have a few verses concerning Leah and we can get an insight into her situation and emotional journey from these.

> Leah became pregnant and gave birth to a son. She named him Reuben, for she said, "It is because the Lord has seen my misery. Surely my husband will love me now."
>
> She conceived again, and when she gave birth to a son she said, "Because the Lord heard that I am not loved, he gave me this one too." So she named him Simeon.

> Again she conceived, and when she gave birth to a son she said, "Now at last my husband will become attached to me, because I have borne him three sons." So he was named Levi.
>
> She conceived again, and when she gave birth to a son she said, "This time I will praise the Lord." So she named him Judah. Then she stopped having children (Gen 29:32–35).

In the Bible names are very important. They are sometimes used to indicate a current national situation or one that is pertinent to the person named, something concerning their nature and future role. They indicate changes in these aspects too. Abram (exalted father) had his name changed to Abraham (father of many). Jacob (he grasps the heel, or he deceives) had his name changed to Israel (he struggles with God). Moses means to draw out. He was drawn out of the water, and he later drew his people out of Egypt. One must feel very sorry for the prophet Hosea's children who were called: Lo-Ruhamah (not loved) and Lo-Ammi (not my people). You can study the reasons behind this in Hosea chapter 1.

In the Bible there is a usually a purpose and reason behind the name given to an individual. Sometimes it is not just the meaning of the name itself that is important but the similarity of sound that it has to other words as we see here in the account concerning Leah. Therefore, its plausible to believe that the names that Leah gives her children are important in helping us to understand this ongoing situation and her thoughts and development during this time. She tells us as much in the verses from Genesis above.

Reuben, means "see, a son" but in addition it sounds like Hebrew for "he has seen my misery." She was miserable in her terrible situation and probably her jealousy had settled into deep sorrow. No doubt the baby brought some comfort and some much-needed positive attention from Jacob. Even after the birth of Simeon she is still unloved and therefore his name reflects this and means something like: "one who hears." The Lord had heard that she was not loved.

The third son is Levi and that sounds like and may be derived from the Hebrew for "attached." She is still hopeful that her husband may feel attached to her as she says in verse 34. However, I think the birth of Judah defines something of a more positive shift for her in her hard situation. Judah sounds like and may be derived from Hebrew for praise. What she is recorded as saying in verse 35 is very significant: "This time I will praise the Lord."

No doubt she is still very hurt by the situation, but she has decided to focus on God and praise Him. This showed a much better mindset and a way forward for her. Sometimes when you cannot change the situation or the people involved, all you can do is change your own attitude.

Why should God need our praise? What sort of a God needs to be praised? He doesn't need it. God needs nothing from us. All the things God may ask us to do, or not do, are because it is good for us. Praising Him is indeed his due and hopefully something we love to do but it is also good for us. It changes our focus and raises our spirits. You will notice how often David, in the Psalms, comes to this position as his way forward in lifting his eyes and in finding hope when he is in dire straits and surrounded by enemies. It is very hard to praise God when we are in these situations, and we may be doing it as an act of will in the depths of despair, but the feelings will follow, and our focus will change—though it may take time.

An Emotional Journey

Recapping on the journey that Leah has taken and looking at it a little more deeply we may find what helped her may help us too.

Firstly, she acknowledges that God has seen her misery. Not only has He seen her misery but has given her the precious gift of a son as some compensation for being unloved by her husband. God has not just seen her misery and remained aloof. He has acted. She realises and acknowledges this, and it must be an encouragement for her. In addition, as a new mother she would have lots to occupy her time and no doubt Jacob was very interested in his first child, so this must have helped improve the relationship. The second son brings joy and again she acknowledges God's part in this. He had "heard that she was not loved" and again sent her a blessing. He blesses her a third time, and she is hoping that this third baby will cement her husband's attachment to her but again it seems she is to be disappointed. Nevertheless, the name of the fourth son, Judah, would suggest that now she is no longer looking to her husband alone for her love and fulfilment (at least not as wholly as before) but now she is focussed on God. This must be a better place for Leah to abide.

It is hard to keep throwing yourself on the rock of someone else's indifference. She has now found some peace in a relationship with God who she knows loves her and listens to her and has given her compensation. An amazing and wonderful compensation. Not just the children but the fact that she is now praising God will give a great lift to her spirits. God is someone who will always love her and never give her cause for jealousy or feeling unloved. He will not let her down. Not only that, but He is much more powerful than her husband will ever be and understands her better. A safe place for her to invest her love and praise, where she can be assured it will be reciprocated. It obviously took many painful years, but Leah had arrived at a better place.

To try to get the fulfilment and security from another human being that we can only truly get from God is unsound. Not only are the people in whom we wish to put that trust flawed and sinful themselves, but even with the best will in the world, they will probably let us down. If from nothing else, just by being mortal and dying. The journey from one state to another for Leah was probably long and painful, and always a work in progress, but it was progress to a better place. Looking to God was a positive start.

A Childless Wife

The nature of jealousy is that it usually develops and grows within families or other close relationships such as friendship groups or workplaces. We have not looked at envy yet but that does not necessarily require the element of closeness that jealousy does. We notice the aspect of loss, or perceived loss, more acutely in close relationships, which is an aspect of jealousy but not necessarily of envy. Just as it was hard for Leah to escape her jealousy it eventually became the same for Rachel too. "When Rachel saw that she was not bearing Jacob any children, she became jealous of her sister. So she said to Jacob, "Give me children, or I'll die!"" (Gen 30:1).

Leah was jealous of Rachel because she was unloved by the shared husband and Rachel is jealous of Leah on account of her sister's fertility and her own childlessness. Leah, we see has looked to God to remedy the situation or at least ameliorate it. Rachel here is blaming her husband and looking to him for a solution, though obviously her outburst was a result of pain and anger, exacerbated by seeing her sister's happy brood. Ironically, Jacob could have done something to improve the situation with Leah, had he chosen to, he could have shown her some love, but there is nothing he could do to solve Rachel's problem as he points out: "Jacob became angry with her and said, "Am I in the place of God, who has kept you from having children?"" (Gen 30:2).

It is hard not to feel sympathy for all the individuals caught up and bound together by this situation which was not of their own making. No-one it seems is very happy or at peace.

Helping God.

What Rachel does next is very reminiscent of an earlier situation regarding Abraham and Sarah and their childlessness. Sarah decided she had to resolve the situation herself and so too does Rachel, and in the same way. She decides to use her maidservant as a surrogate. Jacob does seem quite passive in all the various arrangements with the wives and surrogates as the chapters and children continue. Like Abraham with Sarah before him he agrees to Rachel's plan and two more boys follow on via Rachel's maidservant, Bilhah. They are Dan and Naphtali. Again, they are given names that are indicative of the situation.

> Then she said, "Here is Bilhah, my servant. Sleep with her so that she can bear children for me and I too can build a family through her."
> So she gave him her servant Bilhah as a wife. Jacob slept with her, and she became pregnant and bore him a son. Then Rachel said, "God has vindicated me; he has listened to my plea and given me a son." Because of this she named him Dan. Rachel's servant Bilhah conceived again and bore Jacob a second son. Then Rachel said, "I have had a great struggle with my sister, and I have won." So she named him Naphtali (Gen 30:4-8).

It is understandable from a human point of view why Rachel resorted to this form of surrogacy, but it is not expressive of waiting on, or depending on, God. Leah had had to live with her jealousy and try to overcome it with God's help. Rachel did not know at this stage that she was eventually to have two children of her own, she just needed to wait and be patient for God to do His work in her and for His timing. However, though she has these two sons which she classifies as her own, it does not seem to have improved her situation because she later resorts to other forms of help. This time looking to superstition and the supernatural to resolve her childlessness and trying something akin to witchcraft in the incident of the mandrakes.

These are plants which are considered to have magic properties which will act like a love potion and potentially help infertility. Leah's eldest son, Reuben, had found them whilst out harvesting and brought them back to his mother, Leah. On hearing of this Rachel requested some of the mandrakes. No doubt in the hope that they would help achieve her aim. Ironically, not only does she not get pregnant herself as a consequence of these negotiations but the resultant bargaining between the sisters, means that Jacob is "loaned out" to sleep with Leah, and it is she who goes on to have two more sons and a daughter.

> So when Jacob came in from the fields that evening, Leah went out to meet him. "You must sleep with me," she said. "I have hired you with my son's mandrakes." So he slept with her that night.
> God listened to Leah, and she became pregnant and bore Jacob a fifth son. Then Leah said, "God has rewarded me for giving my servant to my husband." So she named him Issachar.
> Leah conceived again and bore Jacob a sixth son. Then Leah said, "God has presented me with a precious gift. This time my husband will treat me with honour, because I have borne him six sons." So she named him Zebulun.
> Sometime later she gave birth to a daughter and named her Dinah Gen 30:14–21.

In this passage we see reference to an event prior to the episode with the mandrakes (Gen 3:9–13). After seeing Rachel's attempt at surrogacy, Leah decided to do the same thing and had been fruitful in this endeavour also. The names of her servant's children continue to reflect her mindset. She calls them good fortune (Gad) and happy (Asher). Her new children here named, suggests she feels rewarded by God and sure now that her husband will honour her.

Taking time to draw breath and enumerate the children that make up the tribe of Israel so far, we see that Leah has six birth sons and at least one daughter. Her maidservant Zilpah has two sons. Rachel's maidservant, Bilhah, also has two sons. We now have ten of the twelve tribes that are eventually to make up Israel.

> Then God remembered Rachel; he listened to her and enabled her to conceive. She became pregnant and gave birth to a son and said, "God has taken away my disgrace." She named him Joseph, and said, "May the Lord add to me another son" Gen 30:22–24).

A period of at least three years or possibly more must have elapsed since the mandrake incident as Leah has had time to have three more children. We are told "God remembered Rachel." When we say we have remembered something it usually means something has been brought to our notice that we need to do, something perhaps we had forgotten. Obviously, God has not forgotten in the sense in which we may use the word. It is more akin to saying the time was right for Him to act. It is also interesting to note the slight nuanced difference between the way the two sisters are referred to here. "God listened to Leah" but He "remembered Rachel." If you are listening to someone that suggests an ongoing conversation or relationship. "Remembered" does not carry those same connotations.

The name that Rachel gives her first son is Joseph. It means something like: "may God add" or "increaser, repeater, doubler." It is perhaps unkind to read too much into this choice of name, but it does not carry the same thankfulness and positivity as Judah, praising God; Gad, good fortune; or Asher, happy; or Zebulun, honoured; or Issachar, rewarded by God. It's more like: I need another. It was the competition which jealousy can engender that may have caused her to think this way.

She had been longing for a child for years and had she not had her sister with which to compare herself, she may have felt much more joy and gratitude in the birth of this first son. Comparison with others and their lot in life is a big component of jealousy. It can lead us to overlook what we already have and how blessed we are. It gnaws away at us and means we do not enjoy or appreciate properly that with which we have already been blessed.

Household Gods

An event that happened earlier in Rachel's life which may give more insight into her mindset is during the time when Jacob decides to leave her father, Laban. Jacob does not let Laban know of this plan and flees as secretly and quickly as he can. Without any elucidating detail it is hard to know why Rachel acts as she does prior to this departure but she waits till her father is out and then steals his household gods. "When Laban had gone to shear his sheep, Rachel stole her father's household gods" (Gen 31:19).

Why would she do this? These household gods are teraphim in Hebrew and are also referred to as household images and idols in various passages and translations. The link with idolatry is made clear in this verse from 1 Kings. Here King Josiah is trying to get rid of idolatry and re-establish the word of God:

> Furthermore, Josiah got rid of the mediums and spiritists, the household gods, the idols and all the other detestable things seen

in Judah and Jerusalem. This he did to fulfil the requirements of the law written in the book that Hilkiah the priest had discovered in the house of the Lord (2 Kgs 23:24).

Whatever they were, or whatever form they took, they were the antithesis of the word of God. They had to be put away so the word of God could be established. The issue of the household gods would have been highlighted for Rachel just prior to return to Bethel.

> Then God said to Jacob, "Go up to Bethel and settle there, and build an altar there to God, who appeared to you when you were fleeing from your brother Esau."
> So Jacob said to his household and to all who were with him, "Get rid of the foreign gods you have with you, and purify yourselves and change your clothes. Then come, let us go up to Bethel, where I will build an altar to God, who answered me in the day of my distress and who has been with me wherever I have gone." So they gave Jacob all the foreign gods they had and the rings in their ears, and Jacob buried them under the oak at Shechem. Then they set out, and the terror of God fell on the towns all around them so that no one pursued them" (Gen 35:1–5).

The text does not tell us if Rachel hands over the household gods that she had stolen to Jacob for destruction at this time. But the next thing that happens is that Rachel does indeed have the one more son that she had requested of God, Benjamin, and then she dies in childbirth. (Gen 35:16–20)

Did she hand over those gods? Or was she too embarrassed at this late stage? Sometimes the longer we go on in sin the harder it is to repent. Not impossible of course and sometimes we can stand a guilty conscience no longer and are compelled to act. We are reminded of two things here. Firstly, earlier in Genesis Rachel had said to Jacob: "'Give me children, or I'll die'" (Gen 30:1). Secondly, after her theft of the household gods, Laban had pursued Jacob and requested the return of his household gods. Jacob who knew nothing of this theft had said: "But if you find anyone who has your gods, he shall not live" (Gen 31:32).

I am not suggesting that God took the words of a desperate woman that were probably uttered thoughtlessly and killed her, or that Jacob's words were used in such a way either but . . . God does take idolatry extremely seriously. It is a terrible sin especially on this occasion when the chosen tribe of Israel are now going to be back dwelling in the Promised Land. Jacob knew that all idols had to go. He was fresh from an encounter wrestling with God in Genesis chapter 32. He wanted his people to be as pure as possible. Just as King Josiah had when the law was rediscovered.

Achan had been given time to confess and repent. Rachel too had been given lots of time. Her jealousy had initially driven her to try to find a solution herself to her childlessness by using a form of surrogacy. Then she had turned to superstition and the supernatural in the episode of the mandrakes. It was at least three years after that incident before she had a child. It was possible that God waited this long so that she would realise that it had nothing to do with the mandrakes, but as we the readers know from the text, it was thanks to Him. She may have had some faith in the God of her husband Jacob, but she was going to make sure she had covered all the bases and take any other supernatural help she could get.

She is given one last chance before the birth of Benjamin to give up these gods.

It may be by this time that she does not have any trust in them but is merely trying to cover her earlier sin and does not want to hand them over. She is prepared for whatever reason to go on with these hidden gods. God cannot allow this idolatry to fester in the centre of the family. These are the chosen people. They cannot have a foot in either camp. They must be totally committed to Him. As we are told throughout the Bible you cannot serve two gods or be a double-minded man or woman. God is a jealous God!

This is a chapter about jealousy. These matters could be seen as irrelevant side-tracks. Nevertheless, as we also saw with covetousness, this emotion of jealousy can lead us down some very dark alleyways if we let it. In the case of Rachel, it caused her to seek out her own ways of resolving an issue which God already had in hand. Then when she was not truly satisfied with the outcome of that experiment, she turned to another god she hoped would give her what she wanted, when she wanted it. It is the difference between looking to the only living God and consulting Him and saying: "Your will be done" or looking for another god to whom you can say: "My will be done." We see in the lives of these sisters, different focusses for the emotion of jealousy and different ways of dealing with it.

Obviously, it is not an entirely black or white situation. For whatever reason Reuben did bring the mandrakes to his mother Leah, and she traded them. Maybe she was aware of her sister's superstition. She most certainly must have been aware of Rachel's desire for children. Equally when Rachel has her first surrogate child she does say: "'God has vindicated me; he has listened to my plea and given me a son." Because of this she named him Dan" (Gen 30:6). The birth of the second child by her servant Bilhah however suggests a less noble motivation: "Then Rachel said, "I have had a great struggle with my sister, and I have won." So she named him Naphtali" (Gen 30:8).

The focus is not on God at all but on the competition. Jealousy is about comparison and competition. This still seems to be her mindset.

8

Dealing With Jealousy: Human Perception Verses Spiritual Reality

Human Perception

As previously for coveting we want to consider some of the effects of jealousy and how God can help us deal with this particularly strong emotion.

If the cry of the covetous heart is: "I want it!" The cry of the jealous heart echoes the same emotion but with the addition of: "It's mine and I want it back." One of the differences between jealousy and covetousness is the sense of loss. Something that was ours, or that we at least perceive should have been ours, has been taken away or withheld. The brothers felt it was their right to be treated equally as they were all Jacob's children. Jacob's preference for Joseph was seen as a loss to them. It diminished their amount of attention, love, status, and possibly also goods and chattels.

Considering the basis of both statements we encounter the idea that: "It's mine!"

This notion shows how out of kilter with spiritual reality our perception is if we really think that is true. We couldn't be more wrong because nothing belongs to us. Not our house, car, money; husband, wife, children; talents, skills, gifting; body, soul, or spirit. Not the food we will eat today or the air we are going to breathe in the next minute, or the ground we are standing on right now.

Nothing belongs to us.

Possibly the only thing that we could say, with some trepidation, that we do own, is our will. Theologians have differing beliefs on the free will issue but whatever your views on those arguments we certainly own nothing else. Everything belongs to God. When you start to see the world from that perspective it sets a different light on the things we call ours. Whatever you think you own, God has given to you. That is the ground zero from which you should build your thinking. We own nothing and because of our sinful rebellion and ingratitude we have a right to nothing—if God does not choose to give it to us.

It is probably easier to accept that we do not own material possessions. Most Christians would ostensibly agree with that. When it comes to people, partners, and children it can be more difficult to accept. Harder still is our attitude to the things that we absolutely think of as belonging to us, and that is our skills, talents and gifts. We may have worked hard on these abilities, perfecting, and honing them over the years. Neither does this just apply to gifts that we usually think of as spiritual gifts but any gifts or talents we have.

> For you created my inmost being;
> you knit me together in my mother's womb.
> I praise you because I am fearfully and wonderfully made;
> your works are wonderful, I know that full well.
> My frame was not hidden from you when I was made in the secret place,
> when I was woven together in the depths of the earth" (Ps 139:13–15).

You think you have made yourself into a successful banker/housewife/secretary/pastor?

You need to consider that God gave you the essential skills and provided you with the necessary opportunities, training, and education. He created you to fulfil that role. For your part you should make sure you use those skills, gifts, and talents to glorify Him and further the advance of His kingdom. The problem is that we often take the skills and talents that God has given us and never give Him a second thought. Instead, we use them for our own gratification and advancement.

Sometimes we don't even say thank you.

If you realise nothing belongs to you and God owes you nothing, then everything else is a bonus. Had the family of Jacob accepted this as a starting point how differently things may have worked out for them all. Rather than focusing on what they did not have, they may have been able to look at the things they did have. The brothers did have a family unit and that family unit was filled with people with many skills and abilities. Look what God did with that family eventually. All those brothers and their offspring were needed to make the coherent whole that was to be the nation of Israel.

Therefore, one of the things that we can do to try to help ourselves if we are suffering from this debilitating emotion is to try, with God's help, to change our thinking and view of the world. Instead of listening to our flesh and its demands we should try to bring our thoughts into line with God's thoughts and the spiritual reality and hierarchy that exists. Jealousy is created by comparison and sometimes a feeling of entitlement. For example: I am entitled to a good home; a husband or wife and children; an income; food on the table; a good night's sleep. These are all good things and God will probably give them to you in due course. Or maybe He won't. But it's His choice and these are His things to give or withhold. We are supposed to be doing His will. He is not obliged to fulfil ours.

If we can keep this idea as a baseline, it will go a long way to ameliorating those jealous feelings.

Waiting on God

Not dealing with our jealousy God's way may cause us to look elsewhere and cast around for other means of easing our situation. Like Rachel, we may get tired of waiting on God and try to do it ourselves. This much used prayer of Richard Niebuhr gives good counsel: "Father, give us courage to change what must be altered, serenity to accept what cannot be helped, and the insight to know the one from the other." You need wisdom and discernment because sometimes we do need to act to change a situation and sometimes we need to trust God and persevere.

If we don't accept the premise of that prayer, then we may look for another route to have our own way. We look for a different god that will do our bidding, in other words, we may turn to idolatry. The Bible is quite clear that there are no other gods, only idols or the supernatural in the form of the occult, but that choice remains a foolish alternative if we are not accepting of God's will for our lives. If we have prayed about our situation, we know that our father in heaven hears us and He has our absolute best interests at heart, therefore we need to accept His response. Even if that response is no. Whatever we have asked for may not be good for us. Try to remember some of the prayers from your earlier Christian walk that God appears not to have answered. Looking back now with hindsight and better judgement you may well be glad that He did not.

It could be that the answer is on its way, but God needs you to wait. God may be using whatever He appears to be withholding to change you. How are you going to develop the fruit of patience if you never have to be patient; or self-control if you never have to control your flesh and its demands?

When a butterfly emerges from its chrysalis it is at a crucial stage. Its wings are delicate and if they are touched before they are properly set, they will be deformed, and it will never be able to fly. You may be at a crucial stage spiritually and God is waiting for your character to develop before He moves on to the next stage of His plan. Don't try to hurry this process by nefarious means, trying some DIY or fallacious, supernatural, method. You need to be able to fly.

Jealousy may cause us to act to acquire above and beyond what God has designed as good for us. Like its sister emotion, covetousness, it may drive us to break many of God's laws and flout His will. The brothers were prepared to murder Joseph. Rachel was prepared to turn to idolatry. If we do not act or cannot act to get the object of our desire, the spirit of jealousy will be content just to make us miserable, angry, bitter, or fearful. Then not only do we suffer but everyone else around us does too.

Companion Emotions

Jealousy brings with it many accompanying emotions. As we have seen jealousy is linked to zeal. Zeal is the lawful twin of jealousy. Zeal means that you pursue a cause or an objective with great energy and enthusiasm. It needs to be handled and directed carefully. Jealousy is zeal gone askew. Zeal twisted and warped in the pursuit of fleshly objectives. "It is not good to have zeal without knowledge, nor to be hasty and miss the way" (Prov 19:2).

As we saw at the beginning of this chapter, zeal and jealousy are really closely linked. Zeal is a good quality in combination with other qualities and refinements when it has not turned into jealousy. Simeon and Levi, two of Jacob's sons by Leah, had proved their zeal earlier in Genesis back in Chapter 34 regarding the mistreatment of their sister Dinah at the hands of Shechem. They were hot with anger and executed a quick and fiery retribution on the whole community. This would seem to be zeal burning fiercely and perhaps excessively. Zeal when tempered and combined with knowledge can be extremely useful to the Lord. We see that from the tribe of Judah come the Kings but from the tribe of Levi the priests.

Zeal is a hot and powerful emotion and can be accompanied by other hot and powerful emotions, such as anger. We get angry when we have been treated unjustly or perceive we have been treated unjustly. It is easy to see why this often accompanies jealousy. There can be the same element of loss involved. We believe we have lost something, whether that be an actual loss of an object or person, or something less tangible such as pride. Joseph's brothers were jealous and angry and acted to assuage those emotions. Leah was jealous and sad and her route out of this was to look to God, though this took time.

As we saw earlier with covetousness, a step on the road to recovery, involves acceptance of God's will for our lives.

Possessiveness

Another form in which jealousy can be exhibited is possessiveness. The thought process here is not so much: "It's mine and I want it back;" as: "It's mine and I'm not letting it go." The companion emotion here is usually fear. However, the root cause is still the flawed thinking that someone or something belongs to you.

Your husband or wife has promised to be faithful to you and forsake all others and it is meant to be an exclusive relationship, but to let this turn to possessiveness is very damaging. This type of possessive, jealous, behaviour does not merely limit itself to focussing on legitimate grounds for feeling jealous, it often starts to imagine or look for reasons to be jealous. It can also spill over to inhibiting and controlling all the other relationships that a spouse may have, such as friendships, relationships with parents or siblings, even children sometimes can be objects of jealous possessiveness.

This is destructive in a marriage or indeed in any relationship. If you find yourself behaving in this way, then you should meditate on this verse in Job: "What I feared has come upon me; what I dreaded has happened to me" (Job 3:25). In trying to control someone's behaviour and being extra vigilant in watching their every move you may in fact succeed in making them do the very thing you were trying to prevent. In striving to jealously guard your beloved you will merely ensure you drive them away.

This is not love. It is certainly not love of the other person. It is love of self.

If this is not dealt with it will either split the relationship apart or both partners will continue in this miserable cycle of fear, suspicion, and accusation. The Bible does have a remedy for this unreasonable jealousy, and you can read about it in Numbers 5:11–31. (The Test for an Unfaithful Wife). It would be beneficial to read this before continuing. At first reading this just appears archaic, unworkable and in today's parlance sexist. Is there anything at all that we can take from it?

If you do have these unfounded feelings of jealousy regarding your partner, what if anything is going to stop them? How are they going to prove to your own satisfaction that they are not going to run away with someone else? What would it take to convince you? There is probably nothing your partner could say. If there were, they will have already said it many times and you didn't believe it then.

Presumably if you are reading this book with the subtitle of "a biblical exploration of covetousness, jealousy and envy" then you are a Christian. If you are a Christian, then you would hopefully believe the word of God. If God assured you of the faithfulness of your partner, then you would surely believe Him? When you take away the ritual involved in the procedure as explained in Numbers 5 then that is what is really happening. The whole matter is put before God, and He gives the verdict. The final verdict. "If, however, the woman has not defiled herself and is free from impurity, then she will be cleared of guilt and will be able to have children" (Num 5:28). Some Bibles use "cleared of guilt" instead of free. I think this gives a better impression of the relief that the couple would both feel if freed of this terrible cancer at the centre of their marriage. Free of the ugly sister that has blighted their lives for so long. It could of course be the wife or husband that has been beset by jealous feelings, whichever partner has had the issue God wants to set them free from it.

However, in the absence of the ability to perform the elaborate ritual as described in Numbers 5, what are you to do? There are many ways you could bring this before God. You should pray about this and agree on a way forward. Maybe your minister or pastor could be sought out for advice, or a trusted friend. If you both pray sincerely and earnestly God will find a way to make a clear path for you to follow. God is much more willing to tell us how to trust and obey Him than we ever are to follow that advice.

It is not just about trusting your partner but about trusting God too.

Training the Mind

Another method that some people use to avoid tackling this sin of jealousy is to trivialise it or make light of it; just dismiss it as a quirky character trait. No sin is trivial. It is a serious matter:

> The acts of the sinful nature are obvious: sexual immorality, impurity and debauchery; idolatry and witchcraft; hatred, discord, jealousy, fits of rage, selfish ambition, dissensions, factions and envy; drunkenness, orgies, and the like. I warn you, as I did before, that those who live like this will not inherit the kingdom of God (Gal 5:19–21).

Rampant, unchecked, jealousy can exclude you from the kingdom of God.

The Christian life is a battle. You win small victories day by day with God's help. Some of us can be very defeatist about trying to train our mind and way of thinking whilst at the same time being fanatical about going to the gym to train our bodies. You work at getting physically fit, day by day. You do not turn into The Rock, (Dwayne Johnson) overnight, neither do you become like The Rock, which is Christ, overnight. It takes hard work, determination, and perseverance.

As Christians we have taken on board the thinking of the fast food, instant delivery, quick solution, society, in which we live. We want things now. Jesus talks much about seeds in His parables. They start small but can become huge. Continuing the horticultural metaphor; neither do trees produce fruit immediately. The fruit of the spirit is no different. There is much we can do to speed up the growth and much to inhibit it also. So, another way to try to overcome jealous tendencies is to start training you thinking; discipline yourself. When the bad thoughts come, don't let them settle down on the settee and make a cup of tea for them. Throw them out as soon as you can. Don't let them get comfortable.

Take quick action. Think how you would try to prevent a thief or killer from getting into your home? All the security that you would employ to stop them entering your dwelling, especially if your children were asleep upstairs. This emotion if left to run riot could do much more serious damage to your home than any thief. It will steal all you hold dear, breaking, and damaging relationships, splitting up marriages, even causing brother to attempt to murder brother.

Start studying the Bible for yourself. Look for what God is saying to you about strategies that will help. He wants you to be well. Memorise relevant verses. Get off that couch and throw that thief out of your lovely home. Take captive those thoughts for Christ. You may feel too weak, that you don't have the necessary power, but who told you that? Who are you believing? This is what God says: "For God hath not given us the spirit of fear; but of power, and of love, and of a sound mind" (2 Tim 1:7 KJV).

God has not given you a spirit of fear. That has not come from Him, but what has, is access to power and love and a sound mind. This can also be interpreted as self-control. You are not a helpless prisoner of this destructive emotion.

I am sure that you realise I am not talking here about trying to earn your salvation with talk of working hard to throw out jealousy. There is a difference between salvation and sanctification. When you are a baby, you are helpless and require lots of assistance with everything: to be fed and clothed; to be cleaned and cared for. But as you get older you are expected to mature into a fulfilled and useful adult who, at the very least, can feed themselves. You have been given the gift of life, but you need to work at growing up and maturing. Salvation is the gift of new life. Sanctification is about cooperating with God your Father to make sure you reach spiritual maturity. Training your mind is part of this procedure.

Don't Provoke Jealousy

So far, we have been concentrating on the partner who has an issue with jealous feelings, but what about the other person? Are they to be entirely passive in this? No, your marriage is a partnership. Work at this together and God will use this to change you too, probably in ways you didn't even realise you needed to be changed. We would all benefit from more patience and self-control and here you have the perfect opportunity to develop these glorious fruits.

Neither should you be doing things to make your partner jealous. Be thoughtful, don't do things or put yourself in scenarios that may exacerbate the problem for them and engender jealousy. Provoking jealousy is almost as bad as giving it a home in which to reside.

In the accounts of Judah, we saw that his thoughts had to come into line with God's thoughts and that was his route on the path of peace. You cannot have two wills operating peacefully in one body. That will make you a double-minded person. You will have tension, internal argument, and conflict. To subdue your will under God's will is a big dent to any pride that you have. Praise the Lord, it needs to be dented.

From Pride to Humility

Pride is the underlying cause of most of these issues which we are considering. Pride has a very high opinion of itself and how it should be treated. It is unbridled selfishness which puts itself and its own needs above the welfare of other people. It is the viper in your bosom. Spiritual pride is the worst of the worst and the one against which Jesus battled in nearly all His encounters with the Pharisees. Jealousy is just another offshoot of pride. It is not really interested in the welfare of the other. It wants what is wants for itself. Feed this monster and it will grow.

The opposite spirit to this is humility. Humility does not mean that we are supposed to have a low opinion of ourselves, rather have a right opinion of ourselves. Better still, as C S Lewis advised: "not thinking too much of yourself at all." Jesus, obviously, is the main illustrator of this quality, but the human being who bests demonstrates it in the Bible is Moses. "(Now Moses was a very humble man, more humble than anyone else on the face of the earth.)" (Num 12:3).

Coined originally by D L Moody but often paraphrased and re-quoted is this comment about Moses: "He spent forty years as a somebody; forty years as a nobody and forty years showing how well he had learned both lessons." In a nutshell that is a great example of humility. It is about being a somebody and a nobody all at the same time. You are somebody. You are a child of God. Moses was a somebody. He was a prince of Egypt with all the power and trappings that entailed, but after fleeing that Kingdom he was reduced to being a shepherd. The Egyptians thought that shepherds were the lowest of the low. "'Then you will be allowed to settle in the region of Goshen, for all shepherds are detestable to the Egyptians'" (Gen 46:34). He wasn't even looking after his own sheep! They belonged to his father-in-law. He was now a first class nobody—and he spent forty years learning this lesson.

Humility is often described as "power under control." Eventually Moses, was to have access to the most incredible power via his relationship with God. He needed all the fruits of the spirit in generous abundance to cope with the task of leading those rebellious people for forty years in the wilderness. The patience he must have needed, the self-control! The love of God and man all honed over years and years to the point of a precision tool.

Moses needed to know that the power he had access to did not reside in him or emanate from him, neither was it to use for his own aggrandisement or benefit. He was a custodian of this power. It was under control. He was under God's control and God could trust him with the power. Moses led over a million people for forty years. How many human dictators could manage even forty days before they began to wield that incredible power abusively, and for selfish ends?

Moses, a wonderful somebody and a wonderful nobody. A life to study and emulate.

Spiritual Reality

The title of this chapter is human perception verses spiritual reality because jealousy can cause our perception to be totally out of kilter with the real world, the spiritual world. We need to have a right opinion of ourselves and our place in relationship to God. That is really all that righteousness is, a quality which the life of Moses demonstrates so well. It is real humility. This is the antidote to the flawed perception that anything we have on this earth belongs to us.

In addition, the nature of jealousy causes you to live in unreality. It is a form of self-deception. You are deceived into thinking that there is something or someone better for you out there in the wide world. Or even that you are missing out on something or someone that you should have. You may even spend long days pining after something you have lost or think you may lose. Whilst you are spending hours of your daily energy in trying to run and create your imagined world, you are not living in the real one. Neither is your focus on God or other people. You are at the centre of the universe that you are trying to control and run.

No wonder you are exhausted.

9

Any Good Things About Jealousy?

A Jealous God

> "You shall not make for yourself an idol in the form of anything in heaven above or on the earth beneath or in the waters below. You shall not bow down to them or worship them; for I, the Lord your God, am a jealous God, punishing the children for the sin of the fathers to the third and fourth generation of those who hate me, but showing love to a thousand generations of those who love me and keep my commandments" Exod 20:4–6.

We have so far talked about jealousy in human terms and especially as related to marriage partners. This commandment above from Exodus is the third one and it is a prohibition against idolatry. As far as God is concerned idolatry is spiritual adultery because we are supposed to be in an exclusive relationship with Him alone. Jesus calls Himself the bridegroom and the church His bride in the New Testament. This is what God says to the nation of Israel via the prophet Jeremiah:

> "I gave faithless Israel her certificate of divorce and sent her away because of all her adulteries. Yet I saw that her unfaithful sister Judah had no fear; she also went out and committed adultery. Because Israel's immorality mattered so little to her, she defiled the land and committed adultery with stone and wood" Jer 3:8–9.

If we turn to any form of idol whether that be ones of wood or stone or any other form of idolatry, we are committing adultery in God's eyes. It is as hurtful to Him as it would be to us if our spouse took another lover. That is the reality of the authentic intimacy of the marriage relationship which is not to be shared with another person. God feels the same about us, His people. That is why there are laws written in the Bible against witchcraft, sorcery, divination or trying to communicate with the dead, as well as prohibitions about worshipping and sacrificing to idols. If we do these things we have turned to another spiritual source and joined our spirit with the spirit of something which is a dirty and a foul abomination in God's sight. We belong exclusively to God. This is what is signified when He calls Himself a jealous God. He loves us and for Him jealousy is a legitimate emotion. It is a sign of His great love for us and desire to know us intimately.

When we are jealous, we can let it spill over into sin. It is not feeling the initial emotion that is the sin, it is allowing it to grow and take over your life that is the problem. It is idolatry and spiritual adultery. Therefore, in the sense that it demonstrates God's great love for us, jealousy as used here is a positive thing. God really is the only being in the universe that has a legitimate right to be jealous, as everything and everyone ultimately belongs to Him.

An Evangelistic Tool

This next example could also be described as a positive use of the emotion. "I say then, have they stumbled that they should fall? God forbid: but rather, through their fall salvation is come unto the Gentiles, for to provoke them to jealousy." (Rom 11:11 KJV). If we remember that jealousy usually involves an element of loss, then this verse makes sense in the context that Paul is here using it. The Jews have by no means permanently lost this relationship with the Lord for as we see, Paul goes on to say: "Now if the fall of them be the riches of world, and the diminishing of them the riches of the Gentiles; how much more their fulness?" (Rom 11:12 KJV). He is desperate to see his fellow Jews saved and goes on to say in verses 14 and 15 that he hopes to make them jealous with his ministry to the Gentiles in order that this may happen.

In the martial art of judo, you are taught to use your opponent's weight against them to gain a victory. Paul is suggesting a similar approach here. The weight and force of this emotion which we may consider a harmful thing could be used to bring about a good result; to bring his people to a knowledge of their saviour.

Filling Your House with Rare and Beautiful Treasures

Finally, in this short section we need to consider that the base word from which jealousy derives its meaning and that is zeal. That is something of which we can make great use. However, the energy and enthusiasm by which zeal is characterised needs to be properly directed and harnessed. We mentioned earlier the proverb: "It is not good to have zeal without knowledge, nor to be hasty and miss the way" (Prov 19:2). What does this mean in practise? Perhaps if we combine it with another proverb, we may be more enlightened.

> By wisdom a house is built, and through understanding it is established;
>> through knowledge its rooms are filled with rare and beautiful treasures (Prov 24: 3–4).

Wisdom as described here would seem to be the building blocks that we can use to erect the structure of our lives as we would the structure of a house. Wisdom is referred to as more precious than gold in scripture because it is given to you and something you could never acquire for yourself; we are speaking of Godly wisdom of course.

On the other hand, scripture suggests that understanding is something on which you can labour. In The Parable of the Sower, understanding is commended as an environmental soil where God's word/seeds can grow: "'But the seed falling on good soil refers to someone who hears the word and *understands it*. This is the one who produces a crop, yielding a hundred, sixty or thirty times what was sown'" (Matt 13:23). Understanding must be worked at. You needed to think and ask questions and meditate upon the word of God; do some of your own heavy spade work. Try to understand it; tussle with it.

We are gifted the house, but we need to establish it through understanding.

Knowledge in Hebrew is *daath* which in turn comes from *yada* and is the same root word from which we get the tree of the '*knowledge*' of good and evil. *Daath* can also mean skill and cunning. The proverb (24:3–4) could be seen to be saying that it is the practise of the knowledge that God has provided for us, and we have worked at understanding which fills the rooms with rare and beautiful treasures. We have a gift from God which we have a responsibility to make grow and then use and become practised and skilled at using in His service. Like any expert in their field who has spent years developing and refining a skill whether that be from athletics to the arts, it is beautiful to behold. A rare and beautiful treasure indeed.

With the sound structure of God's word around us like a home and established by persevering in understanding it and Him, God can then begin to refine the home of our lives by using the knowledge we have gained to fill it with rare and beautiful treasures. Then zeal can be properly targeted and fully employed in the advancement of God's Kingdom. This beautiful home filled with rare treasures is not for us alone, but to glorify God and to help our fellow believers. "'He said to them, "Therefore every teacher of the law who has been instructed about the kingdom of heaven is like the owner of a house who brings out of his storeroom new treasures as well as old'" (Matt 13:52).

The energy and drive that could have been used to fire jealousy is turned to profitable zeal, but this needs to be accompanied by knowledge to turn it into a treasure fit for a king.

10

Envy: The Destroyer of Joy

Harm—Joy

"Wrath is cruel, and anger is outrageous; but who can stand before envy?"
(Prov 27:4 KJV)

Envy is the worst of the worst of all the three sisters. It is mean, nasty, unkind, ungracious, cruel, destructive, and spiteful.

There will be no final chapter in this section on "any good things about envy?" There is no good thing about envy. Jealousy may have some semblance of legitimacy because it carries the aspect of loss. Coveting is bad because it makes us unsatisfied with our lot and can lead us into other much more serious sins, but it does not necessarily wish harm on the other as its main priority. Envy does. The mantra of covetousness may be: "I want it", that of jealousy: "I want it back" but the terrible howl of envy is: "I just don't want you to have it." Envy is quite happy to see the object of its desire completely obliterated if it means someone else cannot possess the attribute, thing, or person, either.

In Hebrew, the word for jealousy and envy are the same and they are often used interchangeably. Jealousy, with its root meaning of zeal and with that as its driving force is usually considered a hot emotion. The Greek definition of the word which is *zeloo* is an onomatopoeic word that imitates the sound of boiling water; to bubble over because of heat, hence, to burn with zeal.

The Greek for envy is *pythonos* which means envy, spite, to hold a grudge. To experience displeasure at another's good fortune but without the longing to raise yourself to the level of him who is envied but only to depress the envied one to your own level. It is akin to the German word schadenfreude which literally means harm—joy. There is an English equivalent which is seldom used and that is epicaricacy. It is a combination or the Greek (*chara*) joy and (*kakon*) evil. The English definition of envy is to grudge another's good fortune, success, or qualities; a bitter contemplation of another's good fortune.

If jealousy is hot, envy is cold. At least jealousy may have a root in love albeit a twisted and inappropriately expressed love. Envy has no such lineage. There is no warmth or human kindness anywhere in its twisted make-up. It is the destroyer of joy. It not only wants to destroy the joy of others but neither does it allow its host any either.

"A heart at peace gives life to the body but envy rots the bones" (Prov 14:30).

Other translations add the adjective sound: "a sound heart." Envy is such a toxic poison that in the final analysis, if you don't deal with it, it will rot your bones. The Hebrew word for bones is *etsem* which can also mean: bone, substance, self.

As mentioned earlier very often there is some reciprocal punishment for a sin. An archaic English word which expresses this is condign, which means appropriate to the crime or wrongdoing; fitting and deserved. You don't want another to have joy? Well, you won't have any either. If not repented of this sin will rot the very substance of your own life. Everything God asks us to do is for our own good. He wants you to be rid of this toxic, joyless poison and have a heart at peace with Him, itself, and everyone else. A heart that is filled with joy, and yes, that includes joy for the blessings He chooses to give to others also.

Sloth

Envy looks at the accomplishments, qualities, and success of others but instead of this comparison producing the desire to emulate the other, it produces instead the desire to pull them down to its own level or destroy them entirely. It is for this reason that often one of the companions of envy is laziness or sloth, as this proverb from the King James translation illustrates:

"He who is slothful in his work is brother to one who destroys" (Prov 18:9 KJV).

Though old-fashioned, the word slothful seems to carry more contempt with it than the more modern alternative of slacker.

Even though most Protestants would not adhere to the idea of seven deadly sins, it is still a concept which has fed its way into common parlance. The definition of these "deadly sins" has changed a little over the centuries and originally acedia would have been in the list too. Sloth now is usually translated as laziness or slackness but that loses something in modern understanding. Acedia, when properly understood, is a much better term to express the concern of the scripture and is certainly one of the great sins of our day. The dictionary defines acedia as spiritual or mental sloth, apathy. Though it is not mentioned in those terms in the Bible it is certainly described in both Old and New Testaments. "Let us not become weary in doing good" (Gal 6:9).

We are suffering from acedia when we become tired of trying to fight the spiritual fight against the flesh and become weary of making the effort. It becomes too hard to pick up and read the Bible, or to pray, or to go to church or meet with a fellow believer.

Acedia can take two forms. One form looks like spiritual laziness or apathy, but the other aspect resembles manic activity. You will do anything other than the task on which you know you should be engaged. Whether it is not doing the Bible study or doing everything else you can think of *but* the Bible study, you are still suffering from an attack of acedia. You have become weary in doing good and don't want to make the effort anymore. Accompanying thoughts may be: What's the point? The Bible is an old book and has nothing to say to me today? Why pray? My prayers are never answered anyway. I am not going to church because Christians are all hypocrites. I get nothing from it. These are thoughts that slothful aspect of acedia may engender.

Acedia's other face is that of manic activity. This element will take a different tack to distract you and perhaps try to direct you elsewhere. For example, encouraging you to think I cannot do my Bible study now because I need to: clean the car; clean the house; take the youth group out; make soup; train to run a marathon. There is nothing wrong with any of these activities in themselves. Unless we are using busyness as an avoidance technique to circumvent feeding and cultivating our spiritual needs.

Proverbs 18:9 as quoted earlier says that there is a kinship between sloth or laziness and someone who destroys, or a great destroyer as some translations state. This is one picture of envy. It does not want to make the effort to become like the person it perceives as better. Rather, it would take the lazy route and bring the envied person down to its own level. If that is not possible then destruction in some form or other is an alternative route. This destruction may not be a complete destruction of the other person but an attempt to destroy the envied thing, or the operation of the envied thing. Undermining a ministry for example.

It may be that the envier may want to have a ministry of some form but is not willing to put in the necessary time, effort, study, or heartache to achieve it. They resent someone else who has done this and rather than see them succeed they will try to pull them down. That is just one example but there are many others that could be used. We can be envious of so many things!

If covetousness, jealousy, and envy are ugly sisters, then sloth and envy are brothers.

Comparisons

There will always be others who are better than us in nearly every area of life, whether that be: appearance, social skills, morality, spiritual development, professional endeavours, sporting achievements or even hobbies. It is the unfavourable comparison which is creating the envy. If you were the only person in the world, would you care how handsome or pretty you were? What rank you held in the military? What house you lived in? How big your church was? These things only matter when we have others with which to compare ourselves. "Fear of man will prove to be a snare but whoever trusts in the Lord is kept safe." Prov 29:25

Envy is not necessarily based on fear of other people as such, but that we fear comparison with others. We compare ourselves with someone else and come up short in our own estimation and we fear in the estimation of others too. The proverb says it is a snare. A snare means we are trapped, unable to move. However, there is a way out and that is to trust the Lord.

With whom do you think the Lord is comparing you?

Do you think He looks at your Christian brother or even your fleshly brother and measures you against them? You may say yes and cite the story of Cain and Abel which is indeed a tale of two brothers. There is a comparison being made there to be sure, but it is Cain who is making the comparison of himself with his brother, not God. The Lord compares the offerings not the brothers. He sees that one is a righteous offering and that the other is not. He could be comparing two offerings on opposite sides of the planet. It seems God merely wants Cain to be the best Cain he can be and offers him advice to move forward. "'If you do what is right, will you not be accepted? But if you do not do what is right, sin is crouching at your door; it desires to have you, but you must rule over it'" (Gen 4:7).

God cannot bring His standards down. He must bring us up and of course He does that now primarily via the sacrifice of Jesus and the new birth, which of course was sometime in the future here in Genesis. Nevertheless, He tells Cain what he needs to do and advises him to be wary of falling into the sin which is crouching at his door.

Cain could have accepted this rebuke, repented, and moved forward in his relationship with God. Instead, his focus was not on his relationship with God as it should have been, but on his relationship with his brother. It was a wholly unfavourable comparison and rather than learn from this painful experience he decided to get rid of what he perceived as the source of the pain—his brother, and as we know, he murdered him.

The scripture does not clarify, and this is speculation, but possibly the sin crouching at Cain's door was envy.

Building with Bricks or Stone?

God made you a unique individual. There has never been anyone like you—ever. You have a distinct set of characteristics, past experiences, relationships, background, education, time in history and physical environment. Even if you have siblings, you are not the same as any of them. You are not as Pink Floyd asserted: "another brick in the wall" you are a living stone. Bricks are all the same. They are designed to be as uniform as possible. Men build with bricks. The tower of Babel was built with bricks. "They said to each other, "Come, let's make bricks and bake them thoroughly." They used brick instead of stone, and tar for mortar'" (Gen 11:3).

God wants living stones.

> As you come to him, the living stone—rejected by men but chosen by God and precious to him—you also, like living stones, are being built into a spiritual house to be a holy priesthood, offering spiritual sacrifices acceptable to God through Jesus Christ. For in

Scripture it says: "See, I lay a stone in Zion, a chosen and precious cornerstone; and the one who believes in him will never be put to shame" (1 Pet 2:4–6).

Stones are not uniform. They are unique. God is not comparing you with your brother but with the you He intended you to be. The perfected you that He can see and that with His help you can become.

As the proverb advises, trust in the Lord and you will not only be kept safe, but you will also grow and flourish. You will avoid the snares of envy and jealousy and any other snares that Satan has laid out for you. You will not be stuck but moving forward. The ground may be rocky and hard. You may feel lonely on occasions, but you will always have the Lord for company as you journey towards the destination for which you were eternally intended.

11

Envy: Saul

We see this destructive emotion in the life of king Saul. The aim of its deadly gaze was David. It was not always so. Before reading this chapter familiarise yourself with the account of Saul's life which begins in 1 Samuel chapter 8 and continues to the end of the book which is chapter 31. It is a long section of scripture but necessary background.

Until now Israel had been ruled by judges. The prophet Samuel was a transitional person between the time of the Judges and the time of the kings. He had been leading Israel for many years. He was now an old man, and the people were very clear that they did not trust his sons to continue after him. They wanted a king. They wanted to be like the other nations surrounding them. Samuel was upset by this request but took it before the Lord.

> And the Lord told him: "Listen to all that the people are saying to you; it is not you they have rejected, but they have rejected me as their king. As they have done from the day I brought them up out of Egypt until this day, forsaking me and serving other gods, so they are doing to you. Now listen to them; but warn them solemnly and let them know what the king who will reign over them will claim as his rights" (1 Sam 8: 7–9).

God gave them what they had requested. They had not sought His will, but decided they wanted a king. God tells us here that they were still rebels. A rebel is not a loyal subject and seeks to overthrow the monarch whom they are supposed to be serving. Not all God's people, but most of them, were always rather ambivalent about their allegiance to God. They often served other gods and He was never truly king of their lives. This demand for a human king was merely reflecting the reality of this situation. God did have a king in mind for them, they just needed to wait a little longer. They wanted a leader now, one who would make all the decisions for them and be responsible for them. Someone who was visible

Dealing with the Better Man

Saul started well. He seemed humble and keen to do the godly thing and initially had some victories. Most people will know of his rivalry with David, but we can see manifestations of envy at an even earlier stage in his life. His natural successor in due course would have been his son Jonathan. Later in the text we observe that Jonathan and David were kindred spirits and the very best of friends. They both made their name and endeared themselves to the other soldiers at a young age and in a similar way; almost single-handedly defeating an army. Both for the same reason; they trusted God and knew that victory was in His hands not theirs.

The person who really should have been concerned about David was Jonathan, but he was quite happy to have David as a dear friend and we can see what a good team they would have made had circumstances allowed.

The account of Jonathan's venture we are considering now can be found in 1 Samuel chapter 14. Jonathan had one man with him, his armour bearer. Saul on a similar mission against the same army had at one point a few thousand soldiers with him but they had started to melt away due to fear (1 Sam 13:8). He then made a mistake of counting the remainder: "and Saul counted the men who were with him. They numbered about six hundred" (1 Sam 13:15).

Unless God tells someone in the Bible to count something, whether that be money or men, it is never a good thing to do so because it demonstrates a heart that is really trusting in human muscle power and resources and not in God. Saul had hundreds. Jonathan had himself and one other and he went on the attack. He did however devise a means to test that it was God's will first. He was in God's will and trusting in Him.

Due to his action the Philistine army were thrown into confusion and could have been completely routed if Saul had behaved differently. However, Saul made a foolish mistake and put everyone under an unnecessary oath. They were not to eat food until the evening, and they were very hungry. In addition, the forest through which they were hunting the scattered

Philistine army was oozing with honey, which would have given them energy to continue their task. Unfortunately, they could not make use of God's provision because of Saul's oath and were so hungry at the end of the day that they began slaughtering whatever sheep and cattle that they could find and eating them with the blood still in the meat, something forbidden by Jewish law.

What does this reveal about the different mindsets of the two men?

Firstly, we see that Jonathan had not trusted in numbers and in addition he had found a simple way to test if what he was about to do was God's will, then obediently acted upon it. Saul had made a vow, which superficially may sound quite a good and godly thing to do but in fact merely demonstrated quite the reverse. Far from seeking God's will and acting upon it, Saul's vow was akin to strong-arming God into cooperation. It demonstrates a totally different attitude. Jonathan was the better man in every respect here. The soldiers knew it and Saul did too. The unfavourable comparison engendered envy. We have seen that envy tries to bring down the other or destroy the other.

Jonathan had not been told about the vow his father had put everybody under and eaten some of the honey and when he was told about the vow afterwards this was his response:

> Jonathan said, "My father has made trouble for the country. See how my eyes brightened when I tasted a little of this honey. How much better it would have been if the men had eaten today some of the plunder they took from their enemies. Would not the slaughter of the Philistines have been even greater?" (1 Sam 14:29–30).

Why had Jonathan not been told? All the other soldiers knew about this oath.

Later in the chapter Saul decides that he wants to attack the Philistines and this time enquires of God first, but God does not respond. Because of God's silence Saul states that some sin must have been committed and proceeds to find out more. Interestingly before they begin this process of sifting out the sin, he says this:

> Saul therefore said, "Come here, all you who are leaders of the army, and let us find out what sin has been committed today. As surely as the Lord who rescues Israel lives, even if the guilt lies with my son Jonathan, he must die." But not one of them said a word" (1 Sam 14:38–39).

What a strange thing to state at the beginning of this process. It was as if he already knew the outcome and was merely going through the motions to make the killing of Jonathan seem right in everyone else's eyes. The lot did indeed fall to Jonathan, and this is Saul's response: "Saul said, "May God deal with me, be it ever so severely, if you do not die, Jonathan'" (1Sam 14:44).

If you are familiar with the future life of King David compare this with David's treatment of his children who were also his future heirs and—if he had chosen to see it that way—potential rivals. Even after his son Absalom had rebelled, David was very reluctant to deal harshly with him or really deal with him at all. When Absalom was routed and being chased down by David's troops, David had ordered them not to harm Absalom. When David finally discovered Absalom had been killed, he was inconsolable with grief. He was in fact, as his commander Joab pointed out, more upset at the death of his son than pleased at the victory of his army. (2 Sam 19:1–8)

Saul has here the very best of sons: loyal, brave, God-fearing and a great leader loved by his men. A perfect heir in the making and someone to be celebrated and encouraged. Saul does not appear to notice any of this. In fact, it may not be too far from the truth to say if he had not exactly attempted to engineer Jonathan's execution, he certainly was going to do nothing to prevent it. Everyone else could see the situation much more clearly: "But the men said to Saul, "Should Jonathan die—he who has brought about this great deliverance in Israel? Never! As surely as the LORD lives, not a hair of his head will fall to the ground, for he did this today with God's help." So the men rescued Jonathan, and he was not put to death" (1 Sam 14:45).

The soldiers saw all these qualities. More pertinently they also pointed out which commander was the one working with God's help. They had just suffered at the hands of Saul's vow which had backfired on them all because it was nothing to do with God. Envy will brook no rivals and even legitimate and loyal heirs cannot escape its evil eye. It is reminiscent of another ruler who had a similar problem and took a similar route to eliminate any potential opposition. It was said of King Herod the Great, that it was better to be his pig than his son, precisely because he too had potential rivals murdered.

Later in the book we will have a separate section on the evil eye and discuss this subject more thoroughly, but we will see that it is hardly surprising that it is considered evil. It sees even the best of people through the blackening lens of envy. It manages to filter out completely any good qualities that the perceived rival may have and all that remains is the knowledge that there are others who are better than they. Even faithful sons and allies fall foul of its malignant gaze. Saul does in fact threaten Jonathan openly on at least one other occasion and hurl a spear at him to try to kill him.

> Saul's anger flared up at Jonathan and he said to him, "You son of a perverse and rebellious woman! Don't I know that you have sided with the son of Jesse to your own shame and to the shame of the mother who bore you? As long as the son of Jesse lives on this earth, neither you nor your kingdom will be established. Now send someone to bring him to me, for he must die!"
>
> "Why should he be put to death? What has he done?" Jonathan asked his father. But Saul hurled his spear at him to kill him. Then Jonathan knew that his father intended to kill David (1 Sam 20:30–33).

It is interesting how Saul refers to Jonathan here as "son of a perverse and rebellious woman." It's as good as saying: you are your mother's son and nothing to do with me. Even before Saul became enraged with envy regarding David it would seem his own son Jonathan was a target—quite literally!

Lies and Conspiracies—the Evil Wind of Envy

Envy has height issues. It cannot bear to see anyone higher or abide anyone that is perceived to make it look smaller. Ironically, we are told in scripture how physically tall Saul was, at least a head higher than others around him. It was one of the reasons that the people selected him as king. David, on the other hand was smaller. He was dwarfed by Saul's armour when it was offered to him before his fight with Goliath. "But the Lord said to Samuel, "Do not consider his appearance or his height, for I have rejected him. The Lord does not look at the things man looks at. Man looks at the outward appearance, but the Lord looks at the heart"' (1 Sam 16:7).

One of the last recorded things that the prophet Samuel said to Saul was: "'The Lord has torn the kingdom of Israel from you today and has given it to one of your neighbors—to one better than you'"(1 Sam 15:28). "Someone better than you." How that must have rung in Saul's ears.

He of course envied David as well as his son Jonathan and tried to kill him or have him killed on several occasions. However, possibly the worst instance of the depths to which Saul's envy drove him is the incident regarding the priests at Nob which you can find in 1 Samuel chapters 21 and 22. David was fleeing from Saul who was trying to kill him and went to the

High Priest, Ahimelech for help. Ahimelech provided David with provisions for himself and his men and Goliath's sword which was kept there at the temple. We are told later that Ahimelech also enquired of the Lord on David's behalf.

When Saul was informed of this by Doeg the Edomite he sent for Ahimelech. "Saul said to him, "Why have you conspired against me, you and the son of Jesse, giving him bread and a sword and inquiring of God for him, so that he has rebelled against me and lies in wait for me, as he does today?"" (1 Sam 22:13). Saul's perception is totally skewed as we see here. In addition, just prior to this he had declared to his men and officials:

> "Listen, men of Benjamin! Will the son of Jesse give all of you fields and vineyards? Will he make all of you commanders of thousands and commanders of hundreds? Is that why you have all conspired against me? No one tells me when my son makes a covenant with the son of Jesse. None of you is concerned about me or tells me that my son has incited my servant to lie in wait for me, as he does today" (1 Sam 22:7-8).

He sees conspiracy everywhere from his own son and soldiers to the High Priest. He sounds not only extremely insecure but quite childish when he appears to whine: "none of you is concerned about me." Not the words you would expect of a leader and there we see the heart of the problem is exposed. That is Saul's main concern—himself.

What follows is probably the worst of many sins that Saul commits. He has the Chief Priest, his family and eighty-five other priests killed. The town of Nob where they lived was destroyed along with the inhabitants, mainly women and children. All these deaths and the only conspiracy was in his head; it was of his own making and imagination. The root of it was envy. Envy unchecked, unrestrained, and given full vent by a man with the power to do so.

Instead of looking outwards and employing all his energies against the real enemy, he had started to destroy the very foundations on which his kingdom was built. He was sawing off the branch on which he was sitting. In addition, he had cut off his means of communication with God. The High Priest had the ephod which contained the *urim* and *thummin* which were used as a method of enquiring of God. This ephod was taken by the High Priest's son Abiathar when he fled to seek refuge with David. This event made David's position even stronger in many respects. We see in 1

Samuel 23:9–14 that David uses the Ephod to enquire of God regarding Saul's plans and as a result of this manages to make an escape.

Saul was beyond reason. Sin is irrational. He had a final warning of the seriousness of this action when his own men refused to implement the terrible retribution he wanted to carry out on the priests that he perceived to have colluded with David. He had to rely on the gentile Doeg to complete this task instead. He is always referred to in scripture as Doeg the Edomite, probably to emphasise that he was not an Israelite. As Saul was to discover, no Israelite would kill a priest of God.

Later in the sorry tale, now desperate to hear from God, Saul tries to go back and recreate previous occasions when he had heard from God via the prophet Samuel. The problem is that Samuel is dead. Saul resorts to something which he had forbidden everyone else in the land to engage in and turns to divination, using the vehicle of the Witch of Endor. He adds to all his other faults that of hypocrisy. Every false and sinful step he has taken since allowing envy to control him has led him further and further from God and further into sin.

Retaining the Truth

It could have been so different. He could have worked with David and seen his potential and looked at the reality of David's loyalty instead of fabricating conspiracies in his head. On at least two occasions David had a chance to kill Saul and refused to do so. Saul's mind was set on a tram track from which he could not escape. There is no evidence that could have been produced that could have persuaded him otherwise. "Buy the truth and do not sell it. Get wisdom, discipline and understanding" (Prov 23:23).

We need as much truth as we can possibly acquire. We also need wisdom, discipline, and understanding. How much more do godly leaders need these qualities? Saul was presented with truth, but it could find no foothold in his mind. It was blown away by the evil wind of envy; shrivelled in its blast and distorted by its spite.

If we buy something it means that we want it for ourselves or a gift for others. We want to keep and use the item, or maybe even just look at it because it's beautiful and precious. We sell something because we no longer have any use for it. We don't want to retain it. "Furthermore, since they did not think it worthwhile to retain the knowledge of God, he gave them over to a depraved mind, to do what ought not to be done." Rom 1:28

"God gave them over . . ."

After attempts at persuasion and presentations of the truth from various sources God gave him over to a depraved mind and Saul most certainly did "what ought not to have been done." He didn't think it worthwhile to retain the knowledge of God and went his own way whilst giving lip service to obedience to the Lord.

In Deuteronomy chapter 28, there are a list of blessings and curses that may befall people. Blessings for obedience and curses for disobedience. This is just one of the curses listed:

> "However, if you do not obey the Lord your God and do not carefully follow all his commands and decrees I am giving you today, all these curses will come on you and overtake you: . . .
> The Lord will afflict you with madness, blindness and confusion of mind" (Deut 28:15–28).

Saul was certainly showing no clarity in his thinking and totally oblivious to any evidence contrary to his own warped narrative; that everyone was against him and out to supplant him. He was also spiritually blind. Blind enough to ignore his own edict and consult a medium.

The Conundrum of the Antinomy

How responsible was Saul for his own spiritual, moral, and physical downfall? 'Now the Spirit of the Lord had departed from Saul, and an evil spirit from the Lord tormented him.' 1 Sam16:14

In the study of the Bible, it is useful to be aware of the word antinomy. An antinomy describes an apparent contradiction between two reasonable beliefs or conclusions, both of which seem equally justified. A mutual incompatibility of two real or apparent laws. For example: God is three and God is one; Jesus was fully divine and fully human; we are saints and we are also sinners. Both parts of those three statements we know to be true but, how to reconcile them? They appear to conflict. It is a similar conundrum that is often discussed in the issue of free will. If we have free will, then how can God be omnipotent. Both statements are true, but surely, they contradict each other? The problem comes for us because we want things to be neatly packaged and harmonised.

We are paddling in the shallows on the very edge of an ocean of truth. We are told plainly what we need to know regarding salvation, sanctification, evangelism and much more besides that affects us now, but some things we don't need to know and in fact would be incapable of grasping. Imagine trying to explain the complexities of nuclear physics to a two-year-old? If they understood that one potential outcome may be a big bang, you would be doing quite well. Compared to the mind of God, ours is on a par with an amoeba.

If we try to make Him fit into the small box of our ability to understand we will have to chop many bits off which don't quite fit. We like systems, methods, lists, rules, and formulas, but if we try to make God in our image and fit Him into a formula of our own devising, we will make Him very small indeed—not God at all in fact. "For my thoughts are not your thoughts, neither are your ways my ways," declares the Lord." (Isa 55:8).

Having said that there are some things we may conjecture about the above verse from 1 Samuel. We know that nature abhors a vacuum and that we are spiritual creatures. If we are not inhabited by God's spirit other spirits may choose to make a home within us. We may even invite them in.

Jesus gives this account in Matthew's gospel:

> "When an evil spirit comes out of a man, it goes through arid places seeking rest and does not find it. Then it says, 'I will return to the house I left.' When it arrives, it finds the house unoccupied, swept clean and put in order. Then it goes and takes with it seven other spirits more wicked than itself, and they go in and live there. And the final condition of that man is worse than the first. That is how it will be with this wicked generation" (Matt 12:43–45).

The important fact for us here is that the house was empty. The person did not need merely to be cleansed. He also needed to be filled; filled with God's Holy Spirit. Or, at the very least acting in obedience to God's declared will. God's spirit will not strive with us forever. Saul had made a series of wrong choices from mixed motives which consisted of envy, fear, and lack of trust in God. Not a lot of room left for God's spirit to guide with all those disparate spirits contending for space and attention. Attempts had been made to set him back on course. He would not be helped. He would not entertain or retain the spirit of truth and it departed.

An antimony describes the situation where two mutually exclusive truths both appear to be true.

Yes of course God is omnipotent.

And yes, Saul was also responsible for his own actions.

12

Envy: The Pharisees and Sadducees

Envying Jesus

If you are not really convinced that envy is such a terrible sin, then maybe it's worth remembering that it was one of the factors that led to the crucifixion of Jesus. Even Pontius Pilate recognised this was the truth. "For he (Pilate) knew it was out of envy that they had handed Jesus over to him" (Matt 27:18). Both Mark's and Matthew's gospel accounts state this fact.

In the life of Saul, we saw that the culmination of his envy was the desire to kill David and even his own son Jonathan. David was protected because God had plans that were going to be fulfilled through him. The culmination of the envy of the religious authorities of Christ was to order His crucifixion. He was not protected from that because God had plans that were going to be fulfilled by Him too. But how had the religious authorities driven the situation to this terrible finale?

Starting Small—Bat Away the Flies

We can trace this through the gospels and see how their animosity, envy and ill-will grew without check or restraint and finally blossomed into the desire to have Jesus killed: "Then, after desire has conceived, it gives birth to sin; and sin, when it is full-grown, gives birth to death" (Jas 1:15). James is talking about spiritual death as well as physical death, for we know that "the wages of sin is death" but we can see the trajectory that the Pharisees and teachers of the law are following here and watch as their initial hostility grows until it reaches its final consummation in the crucifixion. We first encounter them in the account of Jesus healing a paralytic that was lowered through the roof by his friends to gain access to Jesus in an impossibly crowded house. This account is in Matthew chapter 9:1–8; Mark 2:1–12; Luke 5:17–26. They had at least come to listen to Jesus!

> One day as he was teaching, Pharisees and teachers of the law, who had come from every village of Galilee and from Judea and Jerusalem, were sitting there. And the power of the Lord was present for him to heal the sick (Luke 5:17).

Some of them had travelled a long way to hear Him. They are outraged when Jesus says to the paralytic: "'Friend your sins are forgiven'" (Luke 5:20). Jesus knows what they are thinking and brings this out to the light:

> Knowing their thoughts, Jesus said, "Why do you entertain evil thoughts in your hearts? Which is easier: to say, 'Your sins are forgiven,' or to say, 'Get up and walk'? But so that you may know that the Son of Man has authority on earth to forgive sins . . ." Then he said to the paralytic, "Get up, take your mat and go home." And the man got up and went home. When the crowd saw this, they were filled with awe; and they praised God, who had given such authority to man (Matt 9:4–8).

Initially it is the evil thoughts that cause the problem. A sermon by S Baring-Gould, speaks of evil thoughts as flies:

> There may be evil thoughts of many kinds, envious thoughts, discontented thoughts, profane thoughts, unkind thoughts, angry thoughts, avaricious thoughts, impure thoughts. All these thoughts come buzzing about the head and heart, and will settle to do harm, unless driven away. They are only little thoughts. Each is very small, but altogether they are a great host. They are like flies . . .If you let them come, and make no effort to repel them, they will carry away from you all the graces wherewith you have been endowed at baptism, and they will corrupt your heart as well.[1]

We should not let the birds of the air nest in our hair, or the flies of the plain mess with our brain. It is not having the evil thoughts that is the

---

1. Baring-Gould, Sabine. Sermon: *"Evil Thoughts"* para 4

problem. They will come. It is allowing them to settle and corrupt that is the issue.

In Genesis chapter 40 we read of Joseph's time in prison and his encounter with two inmates he helped look after whilst there. The baker, whose dream was interpreted by Joseph, appears to have made no attempt to shoo the birds away that were trying to eat the bread that he was carrying on his head for Pharaoh. He had not protected these provisions destined for the king.

We will have evil thoughts, envious thoughts. They are the flies of Beelzebub, who is the Lord of the Flies. We must brush them away quickly and constantly. Don't let them settle or soon their comrades will follow, and you will be dealing with an unstoppable swarm.

Rethinking Assumptions

What were the evil thoughts of the Pharisees? They were accusing Jesus of blasphemy because, as they correctly believed, only God can forgive sins. They were trying to square a circle which must have run something like this: only God can forgive sins; this man is not God; therefore, he is a blasphemer. This is logical and, according to their interpretation of theology, absolutely correct. We know that statement two in that thought process: "this man is not God" was incorrect. That was the issue. But surely this was not evil but just a misunderstanding. It required them to rethink. To check out their theology, meditate and pray about this matter. Jesus had provided them with evidence. The paralysed man had stood up and walked home. Why would God have performed such a miracle at the request of a blasphemer?

The next time we see them questioning Jesus' behaviour is when He goes to eat at the house of Levi, the tax collector. They question His disciples, asking why He eats with tax collectors and sinners. "Jesus answered them, "It is not the healthy who need a doctor, but the sick. I have not come to call the righteous, but sinners to repentance'" (Luke 5:31–3). There is of course an assumption being made here by the Pharisees: that they themselves are not sinners. They talk about sinners as a different category of people altogether.

If they had managed to put together the information that they had gained from a couple of these encounters with Jesus it should have been enough to shake their complacency, or at the very least, reconsider their assumptions. They had heard Him forgive someone's sins and now He tells them that the first step to getting well is to realise you are sick; spiritually sick and ask someone with a cure for help. If they had heard His teaching during the Sermon on the Mount that may have helped elucidate further.

"'Blessed are the poor in spirit, for theirs is the kingdom of heaven.

Blessed are those who mourn, for they will be comforted'" (Matt 5:3–4).

All the beatitudes were of course relevant and in fact can be seen as describing a route to entry and growth, in the Kingdom of God. The first step is to realise that you are in fact a sinner and there is nothing at all that you can do to save yourself. You are poor in spirit. On the realisation of your sinfulness, you should be mourning for your sins, and find comfort and forgiveness in God. If you do not even realise you are sick, you are in a very parlous state indeed.

The Pharisees could not even comprehend that they were desperately ill and in need of the divine doctor's help. Pride and self-righteousness were the areas of blockage to the bald reality of their situation, preventing them from looking at some of their long-held assumptions in a fresh light.

God of the Now

Jesus was constantly confronting them with very uncomfortable truths trying to puncture this blockage. Ironically, given all their religious devotions, their faith was conspicuous by its absence. They had faith in the God of their history as described in the Hebrew Scriptures. They also believed in a future Messiah. The past and the future were where their faith was residing. It didn't really exist in the now, in the present; in the only realm of time that it could have had an impact. They did not seem to believe, or at least it was inconvenient to believe, that God was operating right now in their very midst.

Later when Jesus heals the blind and mute man the crowd are amazed:

> Then they brought him a demon-possessed man who was blind and mute, and Jesus healed him, so that he could both talk and see. All the people were astonished and said, "Could this be the Son of David?"
>
> But when the Pharisees heard this, they said, "It is only by Beelzebub, the prince of demons, that this fellow drives out demons" (Matt 12:22–24).

This miracle, together with some of the miracles that Jesus had already performed, were considered to be "Messianic miracles." In other words, miracles that only the Messiah would be able to perform, hence the crowd's question. The Pharisees were now in an impossible situation. How could they affirm Jesus after being so critical of Him? Perhaps if He had praised and affirmed them, they would have had less of a problem in accepting Him. They had to weigh up the information that was being presented to them and compare this with what they had believed and taught for so long, then re-evaluate their own standing before God. It required a lot of thought, honesty, and willingness to change. This is hard work. It is arduous to have to rethink your whole life's philosophy and theology. It is much easier to stick to the train tracks on which you have been running for so long. And for some of them envy had already got its icy tentacles around their hearts. They were making these decisions about Christ from a heart already infected by envy and eyes clouded by its malevolent gaze.

Knowing the Scriptures and the Power of God

Envy encourages you to desire what belongs to someone else, so what can you do to counteract its demands? You could try to deal with the sin at an early stage with God's help and with prayer and confession. Do not allow it to grow and fester until it destroys you or those around you. If unchecked it may even goad you on to destroy the object of your envy, the host of the gift of which you are envious.

For instance, if someone in your congregation has some talent of which you are envious you could try to undermine them. Treat them and their gifting with contempt or disrespect. You could do this in quite subtle ways. The Pharisees were trying their best to undermine Jesus and yet they must explain His extraordinary teaching and gifting. They therefore resort to saying that what He is doing is by the power of Satan.

In some respects, they were right to test His teaching and not be deceived by signs and wonders. They only had the Hebrew Scriptures to study at that time and not the New Testament where we are told not to be misled by signs and wonders. "For false Christs and false prophets will appear and perform great signs and miracles to deceive even the elect—if that were possible" (Matt 24:24).

Apart from the Pharisees there were another group of people who had to decide about the veracity of Jesus—the disciples. They had heard and seen all the same things that the Pharisees had and more besides. We hear them asking questions for clarification on occasions, but they are asking from a desire to know more of the truth. The Pharisees also ask Him questions, but their motivation is entirely different:

> Then the Pharisees went out and laid plans to trap him in his words. They sent their disciples to him along with the Herodians. "Teacher," they said, "we know that you are a man of integrity and that you teach the way of God in accordance with the truth. You aren't swayed by others, because you pay no attention to who they are. Tell us then, what is your opinion? Is it right to pay the imperial tax to Caesar or not?"
> But Jesus, knowing their evil intent, said, "You hypocrites, why are you trying to trap me?" (Matt 22:15–18).

The evil thoughts that they had harboured at the beginning of their encounters with Him had now grown and blossomed into evil intent. The Sadducees too, earlier in Matthew's gospel, had also asked Him a question about whose wife a woman would be at the resurrection if she had been married seven times. The scripture does not state that they were intending to trap Him so it could have been a genuine question, but His answer is helpful to understand the problem with all the religious authorities of the day:

"Jesus replied, "You are in error because you do not know the Scriptures or the power of God."" (Matt 22:29).

One of the main differences between the Sadducees and Pharisees was that the Sadducees did not believe in the bodily resurrection of the dead. You can imagine that this was one of their favourite proof texts or examples to use in this ongoing argument, as they must have believed it made an irrefutable point. Their argument made some assumptions which Jesus carefully exposed. Firstly, that life in the resurrection would be the same as now. Secondly, they had a very earth-bound view of scripture and a very narrow one, expressing none of the creativity, innovation, uniqueness, and majesty of God's ways.

Everything about the Sadducees and their theology seems rather mean and narrow. Therefore, their view of God was mean and narrow. They had made Him in their image.

> To the faithful you show yourself faithful,
> to the blameless you show yourself blameless,
> to the pure you show yourself pure,

but to the crooked you show yourself shrewd (Ps 18:25-26).

They brought their narrow god down to earth and made him subject to earthly boundaries and rules. To them, He was not a soaring, omnipotent, majestic God, who had created the entire universe and was capable of anything. No, He was bound by earthly rules and restrictions. Narrow, confined, small, legalistic, semi-impotent, supercilious, and arrogant; that seemed to be their view of God. No wonder they were shocked and amazed when Jesus said:

> "But about the resurrection of the dead—have you not read what God said to you, 'I am the God of Abraham, the God of Isaac, and the God of Jacob? He is not the God of the dead but of the living" (Matt 22:31-32).

This was their own scripture of which they claimed to be so knowledgeable. They would have learned it by heart as children. Consequently, we can see why Jesus stated that they did not know the scripture or the power of God.

There is a difference between knowing the scriptures intellectually and knowing the person of whom the scriptures speak. Possibly much of their study was centred around the Talmud, which was at the heart of Rabbinic Judaism and the primary source of Jewish religious law. This contained people's thoughts on the scripture and interpretations of it. It is so easy to fall into this trap ourselves, instead of studying the Bible unaided, we merely read other people's thoughts on the Bible. These are a helpful and necessary part of Christian growth but so is making time for personal Bible study.

Usually when Jesus clashes with these religious authorities it is not the Hebrew Scriptures about which they are disagreeing but rather these rabbinic and Talmudic interpretations of the same. This is the case when they accuse Jesus' disciples of breaking the Sabbath law concerning picking ears of corn (Matt 12:1-8) and the clashes that they have with Jesus about healing on the Sabbath (Matt 12:9-13).

Perhaps at some point, rather than continually looking to prove that Jesus was not God, the Pharisees and Sadducees could have reversed the question. What evidence would they have expected and what evidence would they have accepted if they were to believe that He really was the Messiah? He had after all performed messianic miracles. His teaching had elucidated all who heard it and confounded all His critics. If they had taken the trouble to enquire, they would have discovered that His birth fulfilled the prophecies they claimed to believe. What else did they want Him to do to convince them?

It seems they were not really looking for God at all because those who were looking, found Him. They were just seeking to maintain the status quo and protect their own privileged positions. They knew He was special. That He had something to which they could not even aspire. They therefore took the familiar road that envy treads when it has height issues that it cannot resolve any other way, and that was to try to silence Him and bring down His ministry. When that failed, they took the next step that envy encourages us to take, and that was to destroy Him completely. They could not abide to walk the same ground as someone who was far superior to them in every area to which they claimed ascendancy over others. He was righteous and holy; a charismatic teacher and leader; He performed miracles and indeed messianic miracles.

Finally, unlike them, He really knew the scriptures and the power of God.

13

Overcomers of Envy: Nicodemus, Joseph, and Paul

We must not tar a whole group with the same brush for we do have examples of some individuals from this group that did find Jesus as their Saviour and Messiah. Why were they different?

Paul certainly initially displayed all the signs of envy which we see exhibited by the Pharisees and Sadducees in the previous chapter. I am not sure that this was the case for the other two individuals to which this chapter refers. The Bible does not give us enough information in this regard. However, they were members of the group who were extremely envious of Jesus and out to destroy Him. It would have been very hard to step outside the groupthink to which they had been subjected. What can we learn from these individuals?

Truly Seeking God and His Kingdom

Nicodemus came to visit Jesus at night. Some commentators assume that he did not want to be seen calling on so controversial a figure, hence the evening visit, but at least he sought Jesus out. The account of this meeting can be found in John 3:1–21.

> Now there was a man of the Pharisees named Nicodemus, a member of the Jewish ruling council. He came to Jesus at night and said, "Rabbi, we know that you are a teacher who has come from God. For no one could perform the miraculous signs you are

doing if God were not with him." In reply Jesus declared, "I tell you the truth, no one can see the kingdom of God unless he is born again" (John 3:1–3).

Here, Jesus does not appear to respond to the comment Nicodemus opens with but instead answers the question Nicodemus had really come to ask. Knowing what people are thinking, as Jesus obviously did, led to some strange conversations at times which did not seem to follow conventional lines. He often responds to people's thoughts as opposed to what they say. Nicodemus had obviously seen something in Jesus. That He was different; that He was close to God. Most of the other Pharisees and teachers of the Law had also seen this but found it galling and irritating. It was a smack to their pride. It made them envious. They needed to be the elevated ones. They were the teachers, the ones with authority. Nicodemus is prepared to be humble, to make himself lowly. He comes and ask Jesus to explain more to him. What Nicodemus is really seeking is to be close to God and he perceives Jesus knows the way to achieve this. Hence Jesus responds with; to do this Nicodemus you must be born again, that is the only way you are going to enter God's Kingdom. What would Nicodemus make of this comment?

We do not find the phrase "born again" in the Old Testament but we certainly find the concept. They had ritual washing before many ceremonies as well as immersion in a Mikvah, which was for men as well as women. They had also just recently had the experience of the teaching of John the Baptist who called people to repentance and baptism. The concept of being dirty and washed pure for a new beginning was certainly there.

Nicodemus appears not to understand, and Jesus elucidates for him:

> Jesus answered, "I tell you the truth, no one can enter the kingdom of God unless he is born of water and the Spirit. Flesh gives birth to flesh, but the Spirit gives birth to spirit. You should not be surprised at my saying, 'You must be born again.' The wind blows wherever it pleases. You hear its sound, but you cannot tell where it comes from or where it is going. So it is with everyone born of the Spirit" (John 3:5–8.

Centuries later we can be extremely grateful to Nicodemus for his nocturnal visit. For here we gain much information for ourselves about entry to the Kingdom of God. We have had a fleshly birth to gain entry to this world, so we need a spiritual birth to enter the spiritual realm of the Kingdom of God. Even if Nicodemus does not understand the concept of the new birth, Jesus does refer to something with which Nicodemus will have been familiar, and which many of us overlook in our rush to get to the very famous John 3:16.

"'Just as Moses lifted up the snake in the desert, so the Son of Man must be lifted up, that everyone who believes in him may have eternal life'" (John 3:14-15). During the sojourn in the wilderness the Israelites often fell into sin:

> They travelled from Mount Hor along the route to the Red Sea, to go around Edom. But the people grew impatient on the way; they spoke against God and against Moses, and said, "Why have you brought us up out of Egypt to die in the desert? There is no bread! There is no water! And we detest this miserable food!"
>
> Then the Lord sent venomous snakes among them; they bit the people and many Israelites died. The people came to Moses and said, "We sinned when we spoke against the Lord and against you. Pray that the Lord will take the snakes away from us." So Moses prayed for the people.
>
> The Lord said to Moses, "Make a snake and put it up on a pole; anyone who is bitten can look at it and live." So Moses made a bronze snake and put it up on a pole. Then when anyone was bitten by a snake and looked at the bronze snake, he lived (Num 21:4-9).

They were grumbling again. Life on the journey to the Promised Land was hard. Even after nearly forty years they had not gotten Egypt out of their system. Life in the world is sometimes easier and seems more pleasant to our fleshly nature. They wanted jam now, not milk and honey sometime in the distant future. Satan is often represented as a snake, so this dissatisfaction allowed them to be a prime target for his poison. If we adopt a similar attitude of dissatisfaction with our lot, we also open ourselves up as a prime target for Satan's poisonous darts. When we allow envy to take hold it is like being bitten by a poisonous snake: "envy rots the bones."

Jesus connects this incident of the raising of the bronze snake with His crucifixion and resurrection. He was to be lifted-up on a cross and anyone who looked on Him and believed would from now on be saved from sin and death. Sin would be literally hammered to the cross and they could look at it and see that it was now harmless and dealt with. It could no longer poison them. God did not remove the snakes which presumably He could have done as He had sent them in the first place. He instead provided a method to remedy their poisonous bites.

We will be bitten by jealousy and envy; it is part and parcel of living in this world, but we need to look swiftly at Christ, especially Christ on the cross and remember He has provided a cure for this poison. We don't need to let it flow through our system, infecting and corrupting all our organs, making us dissatisfied with God and our dusty journey to His Kingdom. It may seem that the citizens of Egypt have a more pleasant, settled, and prosperous existence but we should not be envious of that. This is not our home, and the journey will be worth it in the end.

Later Nicodemus *was* to see Jesus lifted-up on the cross. I am sure he would have remembered this conversation then. Like many of the others of his cohort Nicodemus could have allowed himself to be bitten and infected with envy. Instead of remaining puffed-up in self-righteousness, he chose to make himself small. He humbled himself and looked up to Jesus, and there he found the cure for all his ills, and his guide on the road to the Kingdom of God.

Courage Against the Crowd

Nicodemus was not on his own as a dissenting voice amongst the general cacophony of condemnation and abuse directed towards Jesus by the Sanhedrin. We see there is another member of the council who was prepared to go against the grain: Joseph of Arimathea. It is important that we learn to think for ourselves and don't get swept along by the spirit of the age, or every wind of doctrine. Or everything trending on social media!

We can learn from this that when we give our testimony and witness for Jesus, that though the majority appear to mock, there may nevertheless be those amongst the crowd who hear the message and respond.

Joseph of Arimathea is mentioned in all four gospels.

> Now there was a man named Joseph, a member of the Council, a good and upright man, who had not consented to their decision and action. He came from the Judean town of Arimathea, and he was waiting for the kingdom of God. Going to Pilate, he asked for Jesus' body. Then he took it down, wrapped it in linen cloth and placed it in a tomb cut in the rock, one in which no one had yet been laid. It was Preparation Day, and the Sabbath was about to begin (Luke 23:50–54).

Mark's gospel tells us he went boldly to Pilate. In John's gospel we get the additional information that he was accompanied by Nicodemus.

He was accompanied by Nicodemus, the man who earlier had visited Jesus at night. Nicodemus brought a mixture of myrrh and aloes, about seventy-five pounds. Taking Jesus' body, the two of them wrapped it, with the spices, in strips of linen. This was in accordance with Jewish burial customs (John 19:39–40).

Matthew's gospel confirms that Joseph was a disciple of Jesus and suggests that it was his own tomb that was used for Jesus' burial. Much of what we have already said about Nicodemus is obviously applicable to Joseph too. He was a brave man who had the courage of his convictions and exhibited this to the Roman and Jewish authorities by the action that he took. "Like a muddied spring or a polluted well is a righteous man who gives way to the wicked" (Prov 25:26). Joseph did not give way to the wicked. He stood against the wicked even though it must have been extremely difficult for him. There is a valuable lesson for us all in his example.

A Diligent Seeker

We find no textual evidence to accuse either Nicodemus or Joseph of envy. They were merely part of an envious group who sought to destroy Jesus. However, the same cannot be said for the third member of the trio, the apostle Paul. He has some similarities with his namesake of our previous chapter. His name was originally Saul, and he too was from the tribe of Benjamin.

He was fizzing with a mixture of jealousy and envy. We saw earlier that jealousy has the component of zeal which can be used for a good purpose when directed and controlled. Saul certainly had zeal. He hated with a passion all Christians, or followers of The Way as they were then known. He was prepared to travel hundreds of miles to see them tracked down. Then satisfied to see them stoned to death.

> Then Paul said: "I am a Jew, born in Tarsus of Cilicia, but brought up in this city. I studied under Gamaliel and was thoroughly trained in the law of our fathers and was just as zealous for God as any of you are today. I persecuted the followers of this Way to their death, arresting both men and women and throwing them into prison, as the high priest and all the Council can testify. I even obtained letters from them to their brothers in Damascus, and went there to bring these people as prisoners to Jerusalem to be punished" (Acts 22:2–5).

We see him too at the stoning of the first Christian martyr:

> When they (Sanhedrin) heard this, they were furious and gnashed their teeth at him. But Stephen, full of the Holy Spirit, looked up to heaven and saw the glory of God, and Jesus standing at the right hand of God. "Look," he said, "I see heaven open and the Son of Man standing at the right hand of God."
>
> At this they covered their ears and, yelling at the top of their voices, they all rushed at him, dragged him out of the city and began to stone him. Meanwhile, the witnesses laid their coats at the feet of a young man named Saul" (Acts 7:54–58).

It is interesting to note that the Sanhedrin's problems were not over now that they had succeeded in having Jesus crucified. Far from it. Now, instead of having just one person to deal with, they had thousands, and the numbers were growing constantly. They had chopped the head off the dandelion only to find the seed had scattered far and wide in the wind, making it impossible to control.

Look at the reaction of the members of the Sanhedrin to the testimony of Stephen. Mature, respectable, well-educated men: they gnashed their teeth and put their hands over their ears and started shouting the equivalent of la-la-la so that they could hear no more of Stephen's speech. This is not the behaviour of a dignified, noble, and serious council but more akin to an out-of-control lynch mob. They are besides themselves with rage; irrational and uncontrolled.

Prior to his stoning to death Stephen had accused them of being "stiff-necked people, with uncircumcised hearts and ears!" (Acts 7:51). Their hearts were not open to God; therefore, how could He communicate with them? They were deceiving themselves when claiming that they were supporting and defending God when they were in fact attacking and rejecting Him. They had heard Stephen's testimony and his summation of their wrong attitude and disobedience, as well as that of their forefathers. They could no longer bear to hear what he, and God via him, was saying to them so they blocked their ears—those uncircumcised ears—and yelled as loudly as they could. Then to silence him completely, they killed him. They were not being driven by righteousness and rationality; emotion was in the driving seat. Unfortunately, that emotion was hate, fuelled by envy and anger.

Circumcision is a symbol of commitment, openness, and dedication to God in your innermost being. The heart is mentioned before the ears here. Our heart, our innermost being needs to be open to hearing from

God and then committed to Him so He can open our ears to hear. The Spirit works from the inner person to the outer.

With his last breath Stephen prayed that God would forgive them and not hold his murder against them. Thank goodness he did, or perhaps there would have been no apostle Paul and a huge chunk of the New Testament would never have been written. Paul moves from a position of hunting down Christians with a passionate zeal to an equally passionate evangelist of the gospel. How does this happen? He was known amongst the Christian community as one who would hunt them down. He was one of their biggest enemies. They had no doubt remembered what Jesus had told them to do for their enemies.

> "You have heard that it was said, 'Love your neighbour and hate your enemy.' But I tell you, love your enemies and pray for those who persecute you, that you may be sons of your Father in heaven'" (Matt 5:43–45).

Presumably the Christians of the time would have been obeying this command. They would have been praying for Paul. We know that prayers of righteous people are powerful and effective. What a terrific encouragement it must have been for this early Christian community to hear that Paul had been converted. We read in the book of Acts that many of them took some convincing that this was indeed the case. No doubt one of the big factors in Paul's dramatic conversion was the prayers of Christians and the witness of Stephen.

Looking back at our study of King Saul and David we remember that "man looks at the outward appearance, but God looks at the heart." Paul was zealous for God. We do not get the impression that he was doing this work purely for his own glorification or advancement, he did seem to have a genuine passion for God which he describes in many places in scripture. The problem was that, as we have also seen: "It is not good to have zeal without knowledge." Though Paul was a disciple of the famous Rabbi Gamaliel and would have spent long hours studying and discussing scripture with his Rabbi, he did not know God. It was the same problem that Jesus had highlighted with the Sadducees earlier: they did not know the scriptures or the power of God. Without the new birth and the indwelling of the Holy Spirit it is impossible to know God and to see the full truth of who He is as revealed in scripture. "The man without the Spirit does not accept the things that come from the Spirit of God, for they are foolishness to him, and he cannot understand them, because they are spiritually discerned" (1Cor 2:14).

Paul knew the scriptures intellectually, but he did not know the God of the scriptures. How could he, if he believed that God would be happy with him hunting down and killing Christians? In Hebrew the word "know" carries the connotation of experience. To know your wife or husband, is to have the experience of sexual union with them. Paul had not experienced the person of God until the Damascus-road encounter, which changed absolutely everything. We see a complete 180 degree turn around, from persecutor to proponent; from hater to lover; from sinner to saint. Therefore, the other thing that may have been instrumental in Paul's turn around was that he was truly seeking God. He had a heart for God. "I love those who love me, and those who seek me (diligently) find me" (Prov 8:17). Paul was a diligent seeker. He did love God and his heart was to serve Him, the problem was he had not realised who Jesus was and that God had moved on to the next phase of his revelation to mankind. Once this had been disclosed to him his zeal was now combined with knowledge and it was not too hard for him to turn around. Though it appeared to be a complete volte-face to the outside world, I don't think that was the case. It was rather an encounter with the God he was really serving, and the realization that Jesus was the next part of the plan.

What an amazing transformation. He still had the same scripture, the same education, the same background but he is now seeing it all with new eyes, even though physically blinded initially! What had changed was his perspective and insight thanks to the new birth and the indwelling of the Holy Spirit.

The scriptures tell us in several places that if you are truly seeking God, you will find Him. Unlike many others of his class Paul seems to have been truly seeking to serve God not merely using this stance as a vehicle to self-promotion and to feed pride. The result of his conversion was that he lost all social standing and respect from the group to which he had previously belonged and indeed often found himself their prisoner—an outcast. He was probably blinded for three days to help him cope with this sudden change and get accustomed to a whole new life and way of thinking.

After his conversion Paul did not immediately go to see the other apostles in Jerusalem but he went to Arabia for three years (Gal 1:16–18). He does not tell us what he did during this time but presumably he was meditating on the word of God and being trained and coached by the

Holy Spirit. He was designated as an apostle to the Gentiles. Just as the other apostles had had three years training with Jesus so Paul had three years training too. After three years he visited Peter in Jerusalem and again fourteen years later. With very little prior consultation they discovered they were both teaching the same gospel. The only difference was that Paul preached to the Gentiles and Peter to the Jews (Gal 2:1–10).

Paul, at that time had only the Hebrew Scriptures. There was no New Testament, in fact he was to write most of this himself later. With the Hebrew Scriptures and the indwelling spirit to teach him, he arrived at the same gospel message as the disciples who had known Jesus personally for three years.

The three things that we have looked at here which appear to have been instrumental in changing Paul are: the prayers of others; the fact that he was really seeking God and had a genuine desire to serve Him and of course most important, the dramatic intervention of the Lord Jesus Christ resulting in Paul being born anew.

The three disciples examined in this chapter were all members of a group who envied and hated Jesus and hounded him to death. Pilate had known the real issue behind their opposition as we are told in the gospels: he knew it was out of envy they had handed Jesus over to him to be crucified. Each of these disciples, with God's help and mercy, found their way out of this deadly snare.

14

Some Suggestions for Dealing with Envy

Confession and Prayer

As with all sinful ways the first step is to admit it is a sin. To confess it as such before God and ask for help. You could talk the matter over with a good Christian friend too and ask them, or a small group, to pray for you. This is not an easy thing to do. Some sins are much easier to admit to than others. We are ashamed of most sin because deep down we know it's not the way we are supposed to be, certainly not as Christians, but we are far from perfect and merely on the road to recovery. Admitting we are struggling with sin is just part of the process of sanctification. We need the help of God and our fellow Christians to begin to get better.

It is worth remembering too that the devil will make use of all the tools at his disposal to try to stop you from healing, and shame could be just part of his ploy. Jesus took all our shame as well as sin on the cross. Don't let fear of what others may think stop you from dealing with this issue.

Avoid Avoidance!

A technique that the world uses to make sin seem acceptable is to rename it, so it's not seen as sin anymore. The first step at Alcoholics Anonymous is admitting you're an alcoholic. It is easy to see why this is important, as the

Bible tells us: "the heart is deceptive above all else and desperately wicked." We cannot pretend that envy is not a problem and if we know we have this problem we should admit it and name it. Shying away is not an option and will only allow it space to flourish and grow. As all gardeners know, tackling a weed early whilst it is young, makes the task much easier.

Another tack that people may take in avoiding looking at their problem square in the face is to ignore or trivialise the issue, telling themselves that there are others much worse than they and its not such a terrible fault. They may even project the fault on to someone else: I don't have a problem it's everyone else.

Distractions may be used to cover up the nagging voice of conscience, engaging in constant activity to mask any unease, perhaps making use of alcohol or medication to block it out. Fleeing from the voice of the Holy Spirit into the arms of the god of Hedonism who may on the surface seem a far friendlier option. As Christians we cannot use these avoidance techniques. We need to be honest with ourselves and before God. He obviously knows about our issues anyway, but it is important that we confess we have a problem and ask for help.

We have seen in our brief look at the apostle Paul that the prayers of others probably played a big part in his conversion and road to recovery and that can be the same for us. We are part of a church family for a reason.

Bless and Do Not Curse

An envious spirit is really a desire to see someone cursed. You are annoyed that they seem to have more than you, or something better than you, and you just don't want them to have that blessing. In its advanced stages envy will even wish to see the object of its gaze destroyed rather than endure the feeling that someone is better or has more in some area of life than it has. Cursing and blessing are opposite sides of the same coin as we see illustrated in scripture. We have also seen that it is important to capture these thoughts and deal with them before they grow from a small weed to a sturdy plant. Therefore, putting these two things together we need to notice when these thoughts arise and turn them around by an act of will. When we become aware of envious thoughts instead of projecting that onto our target and hoping that the person is in effect cursed, we should pray for that individual to be blessed. Preferably to be blessed in exactly the area in which we are envying them. For example, if you are envious because someone has a bigger house, then pray for them to be blessed in that house, to enjoy it, to have peace there. Or if you are envious of someone's superior talent or skill, then pray that their skill will be improved and honed and that they will find an area in which to fulfil and use this skill.

This may be an effort of your will to begin with but eventually it will become easier and more automatic. With God's help the feelings will follow on and from our heart we will be desiring to see that person blessed and not cursed. You will feel better, you will be released from this poison in your life and freed to develop and employ your own gifts and realize your own desires. As a bonus the devil will probably stop trying so hard to tempt you to envy that person because all that happens is that they are more blessed and so are you. It's a win/win situation.

Underlying Issues

You may want to consider the reasons that you are susceptible to envy too. If you visit a doctor, he will try to diagnose the cause of the problem rather than just treat the symptoms. Perhaps you are unfulfilled because you feel you are unable to exercise your gifts and talents and you are envious of those that have the freedom to do so. I expect this is especially true of those who wish to go into some ministry in the church. However, consider, is it really that you are unable to carry out the ministry that you feel you have been called to, or is that you want the title and kudos that you perceive to go with the ministry? For example, if you feel you have been called to be a pastor or vicar then consider what they do. A pastor's role is really to care for the flock. Do you really need the title or label to be able to care for your fellow Christians? There are always the lonely to call upon. The elderly to care for. The sick to visit in hospital. A listening ear that you can give to those who are worried.

Do not misunderstand, I am by no means suggesting that you do this surreptitiously or undermine your pastor, but I am sure he would be glad of help and support if it is well-motivated, and you are mature enough to do this work. You could always start small. We should not despise the day of small things. The first Christian martyr Stephen, waited on tables, and considered it a privilege to do so. (Acts 6:2–6). Is that something to which you want to aspire? Ministry is just a word that we use now for serving our brothers and sisters in Christ. You do not need a title to wait on tables and who knows where it will lead. God uses those who are faithful in small things. Remember it is the heart at which He is looking.

Grow the Spirit, Starve the Flesh

To return for a moment to the snakes in the wilderness of the earlier chapter. We saw that the Israelites were bitten because of their sin. We know that the Bible talks of the fleshly man and the spiritual man. Christians must battle with their flesh daily. If Christians are still quite fleshly and have not begun to build up the spiritual man and deny their flesh, they are susceptible to being bitten by sin. The account of Paul following the shipwreck on Malta may have something to say here:

> Paul gathered a pile of brushwood and, as he put it on the fire, a viper, driven out by the heat, fastened itself on his hand. When the islanders saw the snake hanging from his hand, they said to each other, "This man must be a murderer; for though he escaped from the sea, Justice has not allowed him to live." But Paul shook the snake off into the fire and suffered no ill effects. The people expected him to swell up or suddenly fall dead; but after waiting a long time and seeing nothing unusual happen to him, they changed their minds and said he was a god" (Acts 28:3-6).

Paul was bitten by the snake, but it did not poison him. He had little "flesh" for it to inject its poison into and make him swell up. In addition, he was already looking to Jesus on the cross, in the same way the Israelites looked at the bronze snake in the wilderness. The less fleshly habits and thought patterns that we have the better. There is then little opportunity or space for Satan to inject his poisonous fangs. It is important that we feed the spirit and not the flesh. Whatever you feed grows.

Never Lose Sight of Your Final Destination

Some psalms talk about righteous people envying the wicked because they seem to have a much easier time than God's people.

> For I envied the arrogant when I saw the prosperity of the wicked.
> They have no struggles; their bodies are healthy and strong.
> They are free from burdens common to man; they are not plagued
>   by human ills.

> Therefore pride is their necklace; they clothe themselves with violence.
> From their callous hearts comes iniquity; the evil conceits of their minds know no limits.
> They scoff, and speak with malice; in their arrogance they threaten oppression.
> Their mouths lay claim to heaven, and their tongues take possession of the earth (Ps 73:3–9).

It often seems to be the case that the wicked are healthy and prosperous. They appear to live a charmed life with few problems and difficulties. Historically, and still in other parts of the world, Christians have a very hard time, suffering persecution, discrimination, and much hardship. The peace and prosperity that Christians have enjoyed in the western world for so long is something of an anomaly when viewed over extended church history.

We are human as well as spiritual creatures and it is only natural that we would seek to live a life free of ills. We need to remember however, that this earth is not our home. The god of this world is our enemy. He is never going to stop fighting and opposing us. We know that God is ultimately in charge and that He never lets Satan go beyond what we can bear and that He can also make use of our suffering: "Not only so, but we also glory in our sufferings, because we know that suffering produces perseverance; perseverance, character; and character, hope" (Rom 5:3–4).

Though suffering is hard when it happens, we should try to keep focused on God. We may not know or understand how He is going to use this hardship in our lives, but it will work out for our good and for that of others and in some way for His glory, if we love and trust Him and are called according to His purpose (Rom 8:28). We need to keep this at the forefront of our minds even though it may be extremely tough at the time. As perverse as it may sound not only should we not envy the wicked their comfortable life, but we should rejoice that, unlike them, we do suffer:

> In all this you greatly rejoice, though now for a little while you may have had to suffer grief in all kinds of trials. These have come so that the proven genuineness of your faith—of greater worth than gold, which perishes even though refined by fire—may result in praise, glory and honor when Jesus Christ is revealed (1 Pet 1:6–7).

In the Kingdom of God everything is back to front and upside down. We are living in the tension of being citizens of a Kingdom that has been inaugurated but not yet finalised. We are living in enemy territory on the one hand and in the Kingdom of God on the other. It is one of those antinomies which we experience, with all the turbulence that it creates.

When we do suffer, and we will, it is easy to take two wrong paths. We can look at the wicked with envious eyes because they appear to live a wonderful, carefree existence or we can look away from God and let anger and self-pity be our abode. Neither of these will be helpful. They are understandable because of our frail human nature, but not helpful.

We should not envy the wicked because on the one hand God can use all things for our eternal good if we love Him and on the other, we should also consider the ultimate destination of those who have rejected Him.

> When I tried to understand all this, it was oppressive to me
> till I entered the sanctuary of God; then I understood their final destiny.
> Surely you place them on slippery ground; you cast them down to ruin.
> How suddenly are they destroyed, completely swept away by terrors!
> As a dream when one awakes, so when you arise, O Lord, you will despise them as fantasies
> (Ps 73:16–20).

They may seem to be having a better time of it now, but unless they repent, they have a terrible fate awaiting them. An eternity without God: without His light, love, and company. When we consider their end, as the psalmist does, we should not envy them, we should pity them.

15

The Evil Eye

A Spectrum of Evil

All the conditions that we have been considering have a spectrum. For example, we may envy someone the fact that they have a good head of hair, and it mildly irritates us when we see them or are made aware of it. At the other extreme, we may be envious of someone else's partner or children or career. We may feel terrible pangs of envy when we compare our situation with theirs, and over time that may lead us to take some form of destructive action. It is this extreme envy that usually appears to warrant the term of the evil eye.

This term has been used across ages and cultures. Generally, it is taken to mean the top end of the scale of envy, usually associated with an element of black magic and witchcraft. Possibly even involving rituals to curse someone. It is feared, and a trade has developed to supposedly counter it, with amulets and charms available in an attempt to ward it off. People were frightened of someone that they perceived to have an evil eye, possibly because to some extent, we are all aware of the destructive power of unchecked envy.

In scripture the eye is often used to describe a state of mind and heart. For example: a blind eye, a single eye, a lustful eye, an arrogant eye, as well as an evil eye. You may say that the evil eye is envy but with an added empowerment of the demonic. Something above and beyond ordinary human enmity.

Three Ugly Sisters

A Mean Man

We can start by looking at two proverbs which use the term the evil eye:

> Eat thou not the bread of him that hath an *evil eye*, neither desire thou his dainty meats:
> For as he thinketh in his heart, so is he: Eat and drink, saith he to thee; but his heart is not with thee. The morsel which thou hast eaten shalt thou vomit up, and lose thy sweet word" (Prov 23:6–8 KJV italics mine).
> (You will vomit up the little you have eaten and your compliments will have been wasted. (NIV)
> He that hasteth to be rich hath an *evil eye*, and considereth not that poverty shall come upon him" (Prov 28:22 KJV italics mine).

According to these proverbs, someone with an evil eye is enthralled by money: mammon. Trying to get rich quick and accumulate as much wealth as they possibly can. They will make use of you or have no qualms about destroying you if it means they become richer as a result, especially if they can become richer more quickly.

A man with an evil eye is sometimes interpreted as a stingy man and there is an element of that too. Charles Dickens character Scrooge would be considered the very epitome of this type of person. The genesis of this character is interesting and relevant to our study. Charles Dickens had been giving a lecture in Edinburgh and was wandering around the city to pass time before his talk. Whilst walking through the Canongate Kirk Cemetery he saw this epitaph on a gravestone: "Ebenezer Lennox Scroggie—meal man". A meal man was a corn merchant.

Dickens misread this engraving as "mean man" and this set him thinking about how terrible it would be to have the eternal legend of a mean man. The real character, Ebenezer Scroggie was far from a mean man, but the thought stayed with Dickens and two years later Ebenezer Scrooge appeared in: "A Christmas Carol."

The epitaph of "mean man" would however be very appropriate for the type of character described in the proverbs above. Proverbs 23:6–8 posits the idea that you have been invited to eat with such a person but although your host says the right things with his mouth: "Eat and drink" his heart is saying the exact opposite. He is in fact begrudging you the little you have eaten. His attitude is entirely wrong.

Food is an amazing commodity it goes right into your innermost being and becomes part of you. We absorb goodness and nutrition, vitamins, and minerals from it. However, even a small amount of poison is very deleterious, damaging vital organs, making our blood toxic and in worst case scenarios causing death. The food of a man with an evil eye may have this effect according to the proverb. The bodies way to get rid of ingested poison is to vomit it up. This is the best thing you can do, and the body will often do this involuntarily, which seems to be the case here.

Although the proverb may be using food as an analogy there are things we can learn: "As a man thinks in his heart so is he." How could a man's attitude have a similar effect to poisoned food? It seems he is at best begrudging you his goods or food and at worst wishing you serious harm. Anything you get from him will be as poison, whether it is actual food or some other commodity, even words of advice, apparent sympathy, or empathy—all is poison.

As the ghost of Hamlet's dead, poisoned, father says in Shakespeare's play: "One may smile and smile and be a villain." This quote perfectly expresses the duplicity of our villain too. The Bible tells us in many places that what you think in your heart is what you really are. You may be fooled by the mean man, but God is not. He looks at the heart. Therefore, one thing that we could say is that a man with an evil eye does not have your best interests at heart.

From these two proverbs we see that someone with an evil eye is mean, begrudging, and stingy. It seems at least one element of the evil eye is firmly focused on money. Its god is Mammon, and it hates giving anything away. It wants to accumulate and hoard. The rich fool as described in Luke 12:13–21 was such a man. Proverbs 28:22 tells us that he hastens after riches. The evil eye is fastened on the prize, and it couldn't be further from God.

Worker's Rights

We see another aspect of the evil eye emphasised by "The Parable of the Workers in the Vineyard" which Jesus relates in Matthew 20:1–16. Jesus begins this parable, as with many others: "The Kingdom of Heaven is like . . ." He then tells the story of a landowner hiring day workers. He hires some workers at the beginning of the day, then at the third, sixth, ninth and eleventh hour. When they are paid at the end of the day all receive the same wage. Those hired first grumble; they don't think this is fair. The focus of these initial workers is not God, or His work, and certainly not their fellow human beings.

We may feel some sympathy for them and even agree with the complaints of those first workers. They have toiled through the heat of the day. However, this gives them no right to judge God and certainly not to conclude that He is unfair. If they truly loved God, they would be overjoyed at this evidence of His generosity and kindness. If they truly loved their fellow man, they would be ecstatic that some had been admitted to the Kingdom however late the hour. There should be great rejoicing in the vineyard not bitterness and envy. This demonstrates a heart attitude that is out of alignment with God.

They don't seem to know God very well or be in accord with the purposes of His kingdom. They are working in God's vineyard, but they have brought some earthly ideas about how it should be organised with them. It may be unfair to accuse them of merely having money as a priority, as the wage they were given was not large, but there is certainly something that is askew with their attitude. This parable is relevant to our study because at the end when the workers complain about their unfair treatment, God says to them:

> "Friend, I do thee no wrong: didst not thou agree with me for a penny? Take that thine is, and go thy way: I will give unto this last, even as unto thee. Is it not lawful for me to do what I will with mine own? *Is thine eye evil*, because I am good?"
> So the last shall be first, and the first last: for many are called, but few chosen (Matt 20:13–16 KJ italics mine).

The workers who were hired first are not envious of each other, just those who didn't work for as long as they did and yet have received the same pay. If there had been no other workers hired during the day, they would have been happy with their wage as agreed. It seems that Jesus deliberately highlights this aspect of the parable to make a point.

Firstly, the initial workers had agreed a contract with the owner. A penny or a denarius for a day's work. They apparently had considered this a fair wage. It was the comparison with the treatment of the other workers that angered them. This could be seen to demonstrate a very legalistic view of working for God; contractual, like work undertaken for an earthly employer. God does not behave or think like an earthly employer, His concern does not appear to be about the work at all. His focus is the workers as He constantly goes out to seek for more.

Secondly, as God, the owner of the vineyard points out, He is perfectly entitled to do what He wants with His own money and possessions.

Thirdly, we come to the evil eye. He does not say that they have an evil eye but frames the question in such a way as to make them consider that possibility. Do you have an evil eye?

The Last Shall Be First, and the First Shall Be last

This parable is bookended by two other passages that are relevant: The Rich Young Ruler (Matt 19:16-30) and A Mother's Request (Matt 20:20-28). All three passages conclude with a similar verse which could be seen to link all three pieces together. "But many who are first will be last, and many who are last will be first" (Matt19:30) (Matt 20:16) (Matt 20:26-27)

The Rich Young Ruler wanted to know what good thing he needed to do to get eternal life. (Matt 19:16-30). After a little conversation Jesus tells him he needs to obey the commandments and when asked which ones states the following:

> Jesus replied, "'You shall not murder, you shall not commit adultery, you shall not steal, you shall not give false testimony, honor your father and mother,' and 'love your neighbour as yourself' (Matt 19:18-19).

The Ten Commandments can be seen as dividing into two halves; the first four emphasise our relationship with God and the other six our relationship with our neighbours and relatives. Here, Jesus only refers to the ones relating to neighbour. The rich man can confidently attest that he has followed these. This young man was happy to love his neighbour it seems.

By contrast the workers in the vineyard seem very happy to love and serve God. They are prepared to work all day for Him in the hot sun. But they are not at all happy when their contribution is valued as the same as those who arrived very late to the party. It could be that they are happy to love God but not so keen to love their neighbour.

Then we have the disciples who are serving both God and neighbour. They would however, like to feel they were getting some tangible reward for their great sacrifice. They valued themselves and their contribution highly and were sure that God would be of the same opinion.

We can appear to fulfil the greatest commandment to love both God and our neighbour but still have a wrong or mixed motive. Love really has no truck with this competitive viewpoint and a desire to be honoured and esteemed above others. The parable of the Workers in the Vineyard could be seen as being told in anticipation of the request of James and John to have more honoured positions. They were indeed the first workers and they had toiled all day in the heat of the sun, or at least so it seemed to them at the time. All the disciples had followed Jesus faithfully and left behind their old lives in His service. They had shown love for their neighbor, and they obviously loved Jesus too. We should also bear in mind that they had not yet been filled with the Holy Spirit and were in the early stages of learning about the Kingdom of God and its ways. There will indeed be a judgment of rewards and the disciples will no doubt be rightly honoured and esteemed because they heeded the teaching of Jesus and at the end of their respective lives no-one could have been in any doubt about their motivation and commitment. They had learned to be servants just like their master.

If we are Jesus' disciples, we too need to take heed of this warning and God's advice to check if we have an evil eye. We are sinners on a road to sanctification and will always have to battle the world, the flesh, and the devil. When God reveals any wrong attitudes and motivations, we need to take heed and action to change these wrong attitudes with His gracious help and assistance.

Beware the Evil Eye in Others and Yourself

We have seen in this chapter two different things that the Bible has said about the evil eye. One would appear to relate to someone who is not a Christian and has become focused on material possessions to the exclusion of all else and to the detriment of his fellow man: the mean man of Proverbs 23. The Bible has no advice for this person who has no relationship with God and would not listen without a change of heart in any case, but it does have advice for us. We are to avoid such people and take nothing from them. They are as poisonous and venomous as snakes. We may not understand the spiritual mechanics at the back of this godly advice but as obedient children of a loving father we would do well to heed it.

The second is more subtle and may affect and infect the church. We are working for love of God and neighbour not for promotion, honour, privilege, or rank dependent on any claims we feel we have as the first or senior workers in the field. We need to have a right view of God and His Kingdom to overcome this problem and that is by remembering that we are meant to be servants not masters.

The Evil Eye

The Kingdom of God, unlike the world, is not based on competition but on cooperation and agape love. We must be careful that we do not take the world's view of structure, hierarchy, privilege, and competition, into the vineyard with us. If we do, it will be as poison, causing damage to ourselves and others.

As God wisely advises, check that you eye is not evil, for He is indeed generous and—in charge

16

The Evil Eye: Through a Glass Darkly

Drastic Action May Be Necessary

To further examine the eye which may be evil we will consider a passage from the Sermon on the Mount. Here, Jesus, talks about treasures on earth and treasures in heaven and advises us to focus on the latter. The workers in the vineyard would have done well to take this advice. Just after this statement and linked to it, comes this information about eyes.

> "The light of the body is the eye: if therefore thine eye be single, thy whole body shall be full of light. But if *thine eye be evil*, thy whole body shall be full of darkness. If therefore the light that is in thee be darkness, how great is that darkness!
>
> No man can serve two masters: for either he will hate the one and love the other; or else he will hold to the one and despise the other. Ye cannot serve God and mammon" (Matt 6:22–24 KJV italics mine).

Double vision is a terrible affliction. It means we cannot see reality clearly and this makes any journeys we take both difficult and dangerous. We cannot focus in two different directions at once or on two different destinations. Our concentration and focus on important things should not be divided. We cannot serve two masters, for we will indeed love one and hate the other.

The Evil Eye: Through a Glass Darkly

We need a single eye. Not the blurred vision which comes from trying to focus on God and Mammon at the same time. This double vision will impact on our decision making and consequently our actions. The Greek word which is used for evil eye is: *ophthalmos ponéros*. *Ophthalmos* referring to the eye and *ponéros* usually translated as evil. Strong's says this about this word:

> *Ponéros* definition: toilsome, bad.
>
> Usage: evil, bad, wicked, malicious, slothful.
>
> From a derivative of ponos; hurtful, i.e. Evil (properly, in effect or influence, and thus differing from kakos, which refers rather to essential character, as well as from sapros, which indicates degeneracy from original virtue); figuratively, calamitous; also (passively) ill, i.e. Diseased; but especially (morally) culpable.[1]

Notice that there is a connotation of sloth here which we saw in our earlier study of envy. Disease or illness is also hinted at. Sin is a sickness, an illness, from which we need deep-down cleansing and healing. We cannot heal ourselves and need God's help to do this. Neither is it a case of something superficial and small. To treat it that way would be like putting a sticking plaster on a gaping wound which needs disinfecting and stitches.

> "Her sickness and wounds are ever before me . . . From the least to the greatest, all are greedy for gain; prophets and priests alike, all practice deceit.
>   They dress the wound of my people as though it were not serious. 'Peace, peace,' they say, when there is no peace (Jer 6:7–14).

We can wrongly perceive sin as quite a minor, superficial, cut and treat it as such but that is not the way the Lord sees it. In His eyes we are sick unto death. The evil eye is a symptom of our sickness, our terminal sickness. It is evil in the way it looks at others and because of the effect it has on others and ourselves. Its view is tainted. Only radical surgery will save us.

> "If your right eye causes you to sin, gouge it out and throw it away. It is better for you to lose one part of your body than for your whole body to be thrown into hell. And if your right hand causes you to sin, cut it off and throw it away. It is better for you to lose one part of your body than for your whole body to go into hell" (Matt 5:29–30).

---

1. Strong's Concordance. 4190 https://biblehub.com/greek/4190.htm

We must not wilfully misunderstand. Jesus is not suggesting bodily mutilation. He is advising drastic action to avoid any chance of sinning and having to pay the consequences of that sin. Though I do not believe that this was the main intent or purpose of the passage, the effect of cutting out one eye would indeed lead you to have a single eye. That is probably part of the point, you should not leave yourself with any options to sin, as far as is possible. If you are on a diet, you would be foolish to fill your house with cakes, biscuits, and sweets. If you have a problem with alcohol don't have it in your home. If you feel in danger of committing adultery, then confess all and run out of the situation as quickly as you can. Remember Joseph, who ran out of the presence of Potiphar's wife.

Living in the Light

We have seen here that the evil eye can lead to double vision, trying to serve God and Mammon. There are other things that we can learn from this study too. God created eyes. We are blessed by them to behold the beauty of His world and word, but like most things that can be used for good they can cause us to sin too. As Matthew 6:22 tells us another effect of an evil eye can be spiritual darkness: "'If therefore the light that is in thee be darkness, how great is that darkness!'" It seems strangely worded here. How can light be darkness? They are opposite states. How could we not know that what we perceive to be light is in fact darkness?

The new birth brings with it new eyes and new sight. Prior to your conversion you may have viewed some things as good and wholesome that you now see as having something of the night about them. For example, you may have seen astrology as a good tool to use for predicting and therefore preparing for the future. Now you see it as a much more sinister practice because you have now had a true light shone upon it. The occult means hidden and some of these occult practises have now been revealed to you for what they really are. The veil has been torn away. Previously you had been in darkness; spiritual darkness. That world had been concealed from you, now it is revealed, and you see the ugly face behind the mask.

We may fear darkness, but we may also feel that it can cover and hide us. Nothing could be further from the truth.

> "If I say, "Surely the darkness will hide me and the light become night around me," even the darkness will not be dark to you; the

night will shine like the day, for darkness is as light to you" (Ps 139:11–12).

Everything is uncovered and laid bare before the Lord. Darkness will not cover us from His piercing view. Neither will the spiritual darkness of our own making hide us. All our deeds and thoughts are laid before Him as plain as day. The lens through which we view the world is determined by our beliefs and we tend to interpret evidence in the light of those beliefs. No-one is neutral, everyone is biased. I am a Christian, so I interpret the world through that lens. An atheist would interpret events in the world according to their belief that there is no god. In practise how does this look?

Imagine in our workplace a colleague that both I and the atheist know is diagnosed with terminal cancer. In any conversations with that sick person how would our attitudes and conversations with that person differ? I believe in eternal life and would therefore hopefully be able to inject something of that hope and knowledge into any talks I may have with them. I would at the very least be able to pray for them. In conversation with the same person what would the attitude and impact of the atheist be? They do not believe in God, or the supernatural, or an afterlife, so any talks that they have may centre around palliative care or getting the most out of their last few months on this earth. I would also advocate those actions as well. However, I would be prioritising putting relationships with God and others right; putting their house in order as a good use of their remaining time, not necessarily trying to take a last trip to Bali or see Niagara Falls or any other bucket list experience that they may wish to fulfil. There is nothing wrong with these things but when time is short it is necessary to get your priorities right. Our differing viewpoints and beliefs would greatly affect how we interacted with this sick person. They would impact on every element of contact with them from our body language to conversations and obviously any spiritual impact that may result too. Very best and worst-case scenarios could be the difference between an eternal life lived with God or one without Him. With even the best of intentions the atheists influence could be eternally catastrophic.

The Bible clearly tells us that the unbeliever does not see the spiritual world. The apostle Paul, in his first letter to the Corinthians, says that even Christians only see God as through a glass darkly. The unbeliever sees Him not at all, so how great must their darkness be? The darkness that they have inside is the lens through which they view the world. What could be more evil than a bias which leads someone to eternal separation from God?

Three Ugly Sisters

Using the Darkness

We have been talking here about unintentional consequences. The atheist does not intend to spiritually mislead anyone. How can they? They don't believe in a spiritual dimension of life. They are what Jesus would call "a blind guide." However, perhaps a more sinister and potentially dangerous person is someone who is well aware of the spiritual realm and the powers available there but intends to use that power for ill. I think this is what we usually have in mind when we use the term, the evil eye. We imagine someone imbued with the power of black magic turning that power loose on us to do harm.

Fairy tales and folk tales are full of such creatures who can curse others at the behest of an aggrieved party or for their own purposes. Indeed, if seeming bad luck befell an individual or a community prior to the age of the enlightenment it was often thought that the individual or community had been cursed. Quite literally a witch hunt would ensue. Even today, many societies, cultures and cults still believe in the effectiveness of a curse. There is money to be made on both sides of the divide: from offering to curse people and equally by offering to protect them from a curse. As Christians we do not need to fear such spiritual attacks. There are many Bible verses that assure us that God is protecting us from such things, not least: "As a fluttering sparrow or a darting swallow, so an undeserved curse does not come to rest" (Prov 26:2). Birds of the air can be seen as emissaries of Satan, but they can get no purchase anywhere upon us when God is protecting us. This proverb is encouraging at many levels because sometimes we can curse others unintentionally by saying negative things about them, or to them, which may settle in their head like a bird in a tree and have a detrimental effect.

I am sure that you can remember some negative remarks which people have made in the past, either to you or about you, which have acted like curses because they have settled and nested in your mind. Whether we feel we have been cursed or if we realize we may have cursed others we do not need to live in that darkness of fear or guilt, we have a person to whom we can turn to help.

We also have the example of Balaam, the diviner, who was employed by Balak to curse the Israelites: "and they hired Balaam son of Beor from Pethor in Aram Naharaim to pronounce a curse on you. However, the Lord your God would not listen to Balaam but turned the curse into a blessing for you, because the Lord your God loves you" (Deut 23:4–5).

We do not need to fear the evil eye and we do not need to wear any amulets or charms to protect us. The Lord our God is our shield from such things. We may currently only see through a glass darkly, but our God has full clear vision and the power to protect us from all evil.

Help to be Clean

However, what if instead of being the potential victims of the evil eye, we are in fact the perpetrators? We find ourselves looking at someone and hoping that they will be cursed. It is unlikely that we should use the word cursed but we are nevertheless hoping some harm or misfortune will befall them. We need to remember how we started this section with a quote from Proverbs 23:7: "as a man thinks in his heart so is he." We are what we think. Jesus reiterates the same thought when speaking to the Pharisees:

> And he said, "That which cometh out of the man, that defileth the man. For from within, out of the heart of men, proceed evil thoughts, adulteries, fornications, murders, thefts, covetousness, wickedness, deceit, lasciviousness, *an evil eye,* blasphemy, pride, foolishness: All these evil things come from within, and defile the man" (Mark 7:20–23 KJV italics mine).

The Pharisees had criticised Jesus for not making sure His disciples performed all the ceremonial washing procedures before eating. Jesus' response to this criticism was to call them hypocrites because they were obeying laws that had been invented by men but not keeping the commands of God. He said they were superficially clean on the outside but dirty on the inside. He listed the conditions which made them dirty, one of them was an evil eye. Jesus' advice is that we need the inside of the cup cleaned. We do this with His help. His sacrifice can cleanse us from all sin and our ongoing sanctification will happen by the washing in the word. With prayer and with ongoing reading and study of the Bible we can, with God's help, root out these evil thoughts.

We need not fear the evil eye whether directed at us or when we find it within us.

We need not fear it, but neither should we ignore it.

17

Gleanings

This has in many ways been an artificial task to try to separate covetousness, jealousy, and envy. We have seen that they are closely linked and can morph from one to another. However, there are some distinct features which can be seen in each one and examining them in this way can draw out these distinctions and hopefully help us deal with them. This last chapter comprises ideas that may relate to one or other of the conditions discussed and contains a few final views to consider.

Provoking Jealousy and Envy

We have partly focused so far on being the object of someone's envy or jealousy, but can we stoke envious or jealous feelings in others and are we culpable if we do this deliberately, or even unwittingly? In Kings 2:20:12–19, we read the account of the envoys from the King of Babylon who came to visit Hezekiah after his illness.

> Hezekiah received the messengers and showed them all that was in his storehouses—the silver, the gold, the spices, and the fine oil— his armoury and everything found among his treasures. There was nothing in his palace or in all his kingdom that Hezekiah did not show them (2 Kgs 20:13).

There could be many reasons why Hezekiah displayed his wealth: pride, courtesy, naivety, the envoys may even have asked to see something, and Hezekiah had proceeded to show them everything. The scripture does not make his motive clear, but it appears that he was boasting and somewhat proud. (A parallel account in 2 Chronicles speaks of his pride.) It does say that there was nothing in all his kingdom that he did not show them. This may mean he even showed them inside the temple, though this was forbidden and could be a possible explanation for what happened next. The Lord via the prophet Isaiah rebukes Hezekiah for this foolish act and tells him that everything the Babylonians had been shown would eventually be carried off to Babylon and we see this happen later in 2 Kings chapter 25. This does include treasures housed in the temple and would suggest Hezekiah had indeed shown the envoys these things too. What can we learn from this?

This was obviously not the main reason the Babylonians invaded nearly two hundred years later, carried off the treasures and the Israelites themselves into captivity but it certainly provided a partial motive. Being boastful and proud, showing all your possessions to anyone may engender covetousness, or envy. It may provoke people to some form of action to take these things from you, or even just wish ill upon you. The Bible warns against pride and boastfulness. You should not wish to kindle damaging emotions in another. This is not a loving thing to do. We should carefully consider our motivations and actions and the effect they may have on others. This does not only apply to physical things. We should be good custodians too of spiritual treasures that the Lord has given into our keeping. We should not be parading or hawking our wares. In the account about Hezekiah, it seems the fact that the Babylonians had seen these things gave them some rights over them. There is something of the evil eye in this whole account.

For our part, I think it encourages us not to promote covetousness in others and certainly we should be good stewards of any spiritual treasures to which the Lord has entrusted us. We are not to cast our pearls before swine for a very good reason. "'Do not give dogs what is sacred; do not throw your pearls to pigs. If you do, they may trample them under their feet, and turn and tear you to pieces'" (Matt 7:6). Both dogs and pigs are unclean animals in Jewish theology. This is symbolic of giving the holy things of God to unbelievers. Hezekiah it seems, had done this. Just unveiling these treasures of God to others was a harmful thing for him to do. Might we do similar things? Even if it is out of innocence and naivety.

In these days of social media and people seeking their fifteen minutes of fame we can easily lose sight of what we should share and what we should not. It seems the spirit of discernment is not being exercised as wisely as it could be. Sometimes God does speak to us in a whisper and that information or revelation may just be for us and not something that we should broadcast to the whole world. Possibly if we are not careful with His pearls, He may not share them with us anymore. We need to be circumspect about what we share and with whom. Some things that God tells us will not be for the general consumption of the world outside the church. Even inside the church we should be sensitive. It is easy to make less mature believers, or weak believers as Paul refers to them, feel inadequate and maybe even jealous (Romans 14). This is not loving our brother or sister in Christ. We are to build them up and not make them feel inferior by flaunting any spiritual gifting or insight that we may have.

Hezekiah was displaying his physical treasures of precious gems and materials. He probably saw no harm in it and could have no understanding of the potential long-term consequences. Let's learn by his mistake. The gospel message is for all and should be proclaimed to all the world but not all things from God fall into that category. Real spiritual discernment is a necessary gift required in this regard, not an optional extra.

Motivation

It would also be beneficial to consider if there is some underlying root cause to all these issues that we have examined in this book that would help us work on overcoming them more successfully. The righteous person has a right relationship with God in that he understands who God is and how he stands in relation to God. Humility is the attitude required here. The opposite attitude to one of humility is that of pride. In simple terms, when we are humble, we know that God is Lord and we are His subjects and our hearts, thoughts and actions try to reflect this reality. When pride is in our heart it is all about us. We are the centre of our universe; we must be top dog and all our desires and ambitions need to be fulfilled. Unsurprisingly, this attitude is even present in church, where the chief aim of man may cease to be to glorify God but to glorify man, whether it is the individual themselves or humanity collectively. That was one of the motivations for building the tower of Babel. Pride wants to put itself first and its god is Mammon or the world.

> Do not love the world or anything in the world. If anyone loves the world, love for the Father is not in him. For everything in the world—the cravings of sinful man, the lust of his eyes, and the

boasting of what he has and does—comes not from the Father but from the world. The world and its desires pass away, but the man who does the will of God lives forever" (1 John 2:15-17).

Pride can hide itself under many guises. It can outwardly appear altruistic, sympathetic, empathetic; speak softly and kindly; speak biblically and lovingly, but still be serving its master which is self not God. Sometimes the praise and gratitude of man can mean so much more to us than pleasing God. No wonder God reminds us that the glory should go to Him. Partly because it is for our own benefit to help keep that dangerous pride at bay.

Conversely sometimes when serving God, we can appear far from sympathetic and kind. On occasions Jesus could appear harsh and unfeeling. Motivation is key. Motivation which is rooted in genuine love of God and man is the important factor. This is not always visible to other people but is known to God.

The Antidote to Pride

Pride, and love of the world is an underlying issue in all these sinful attitudes we have examined. There is nothing intrinsically wrong in most of the things in the world but anything that becomes more important than God is going to be problematic no matter how we may try to dress it up in spiritual garb. The antidote to these ills that afflict our spirit is love, agape love, as perfectly described by the Apostle Paul in 1 Corinthians Chapter 13. He describes this state by describing what love is and what it is not.

> Love is patient, love is kind. It does not envy, it does not boast, it is not proud. It is not rude, it is not self-seeking, it is not easily angered, it keeps no record of wrongs. Love does not delight in evil but rejoices with the truth. It always protects, always trusts, always hopes, always perseveres. Love never fails (1 Cor 13:4-8).

The translation for pride that the King James uses is "puffed-up." That gives such a good picture of what pride does to us. Like the yeast of the Pharisees which Jesus warned about, pride puffs us up. It tries to make itself big sometimes even by pretending it is in fact attempting to make itself small. It's the worm at the centre of the apple. Very often unseen but it will eventually make its presence known. As Paul explains we can boast about our achievements, albeit in a Uriah Heep, "ever-so-humble way." We can be envious or jealous of others who we perceive to be bigger than ourselves.

This can make us rude and offensive as we try to put others down. Pride is indeed self-seeking and easily angered because it must constantly defend itself against perceived attacks that may attempt to deflate it. Sadly, as we have also seen, it does delight in evil. In fact, it very often wishes evil upon others, even going so far as to curse them.

Pride is at the bottom of all these things and accounts for our love of Mammon as we seek to surround ourselves with objects or people who may help bolster this pride. We like to be puffed up with stuff, including the praises of men. This is very ephemeral and illusory as we can find out to our cost. The remedy to this poison is love. Love of God and love of man. With this attitude in place God is at the centre of our heart not ourselves. It encourages us to be patient, kind, forgiving and truthful. It does not seek to deflate others but protect them. Its trust and hope are in God, not self, and it keeps on keeping on—it perseveres. In short as Paul so succinctly puts it: "Love never fails." As pride is at the bottom of so much of what we have considered in this book, so love is the remedy.

Group-Envy

So far, we have been considering envy or jealousy on an individual basis, but it can also infect groups of people; even nations can have this heart attitude though it may manifest itself under various guises. Similarly with class systems or structures. The uneducated may envy the educated; the poor the rich; the lower class the upper class; and so-on and so-forth. We need to be aware of this and repent of this individually if we feel our nation or institute is guilty of such attitudes. Repentance means we will turn away from this sin which is so damaging and quite ugly to behold. Nicodemus was a member of an organisation that suffered from envy regarding their view of Jesus, but he did not bow to this majority perception and managed to keep aloof and free himself from this snare.

It could be said that some antisemitism though displayed and enacted as hate and contempt, has at its root an element of envy. This may be sub-conscious and fuelled by spiritual forces. Nevertheless, it is a heavy burden to be God's chosen people as well as a great privilege and responsibility. This is not a designation that is going to endear you to the rest of the world—even if it is true! As we have said already the evil eye hates anything that claims to be higher than itself. It would be difficult to have a higher claim than being the chosen of God. This is a complicated topic and a gross over-simplification to boil it down to just a spirit of envy, but it is possibly one of the factors which has led to the otherwise inexplicable persecution of the Jews by so many other peoples of the world over such a long period of time.

Trinity of Holiness

In this book we have looked at a trinity of evil attitudes: covetousness, jealousy, and envy, so finally it would do us good to consider a trinity of holy attitudes: "And now these three remain: faith, hope and love. But the greatest of these is love" (1 Cor 13:13). We have already said much about love but what about the other two facets that Paul mentions here?

Faith is quite difficult to define, at least the biblical understanding of faith. A whole book could be written on this topic alone because there are several different elements to faith, and it is used in different ways in different contexts. For example, we know that there is saving faith, but the apostle Paul also talks about the "gift of faith" in 1 Corinthians chapter 12 verse 9. There is not the time or space to examine the many nuances of meaning here. We need a working definition to aid our comprehension. The Bible gives its own definition in the book of Hebrews: "Now faith is being sure of what we hope for and certain of what we do not see" (Heb 11:1).

If faith is a difficult word to define, hope can be even harder. Language is not a static thing words change meaning over time or are given totally new meanings as for example: gay, hack, awful, fantastic. Hope is a word that has suffered from just such a change. Currently, if I said "I hoped" something was going to happen, it carries with it a sense of uncertainty. In other words, I believe that it may or may not happen. I'm hoping it will, but it might just as easily not. Originally, and in the biblical sense, hope means that something is absolutely going to happen—but it will be at some time in the future. That's why we have a sure and certain hope. We have a hope of Christ's return. That is not expressing uncertainty; it is talking of a definite future event. It has not yet happened but in the meantime, we trust the word of God which tells us it will.

Therefore, hope is having faith in a certain future event which we wait for with anticipation. However, the certainty of this future event requires us to trust that it is indeed going to happen which really means we need to have trust in the integrity of the source. We must be convinced that the object of this hope has a rock-solid dependability; this is where faith and trust come into play. One way of defining faith in its simplest terms is trusting God. To have the sort of confidence that we could stake our life and eternal future on something or someone. As Christians we believe that Jesus is the only person in whom we can safely put our hope and faith.

If we indulge in covetousness, envy, and jealousy, it is symptomatic of the fact that possibly we do not trust God. We feel the need to do-it-ourselves because we cannot rely on Him to have our best interests at heart. It may also be indicative of a failure to really believe in these wonderful future events. It is a failure of hope. We want to have what we want now, not sometime in the future; a future which may be a long time coming and we are not too sure is going to materialise.

In this very brief look at our trinity of holy attributes we can see how important they are to our everyday walk with Christ, but especially important in helping us combat whatever current temptation is trying to attack us.

Not a Christian?

There is an assumption throughout the book that the readership will be those who are already committed Christians. If you are not, then some of the advice given here may seem unhelpful, confusing, ineffectual, and possibly idiotic.

The word gospel means "good news." However, it is only good news when you have properly understood the full import of the bad news. The bad news is that because of our wrongdoings of thought, word, and deed, we are all under a death sentence. The Bible says that "the wages of sin is death." However, physical death is not the end. Everyone will also live again eternally somewhere. This will either be with God, or without Him. We are currently separated from a holy God by our sinfulness. In this woeful sinful condition, we would not be able to be in His presence for a moment without burning to a cinder under the weight of this holiness. Here on earth, we have a justice system which is imperfect, and crimes can go unpunished, but this will not be the case in the eternal law courts. Everything that you have done, said or thought will have to be brought out into the light, judged, and paid for. Otherwise, this would not be a just universe. God is a God of justice.

Most people, even those who are not yet Christian, will accept that they have not always behaved as they should to their neighbour. That they have lied, cheated, had adulterous or murderous thoughts. However, not many consider that they have not only sinned against their fellow human being, but they have offended, hurt, and sinned against God too. Jesus came to pay the penalty for all the wrongs we have committed against both man and God. Thus enabling our charge sheet to be cleared so that we can enjoy a relationship with God now and live eternally in His kingdom.

We need to understand the perilous situation in which we find ourselves; confess our sins and accept the free offer of salvation that is a result of a belief in Christ and His sacrifice in our place. A simple way to explain this may be to say that we repent of our sins, believe in Christ's sacrifice, and receive the Holy Spirit. The powerful indwelling of the Holy Spirit and the resultant new birth is what will enable you to eventually be able to stand before a holy God, survive, and be welcomed into His kingdom. It is just as essential to your remaining life here on earth too. You will only be able to change and grow with God's help. This process of change is known as sanctification, and that's what is at the heart of this book. It simply means that you will be helped to change and grow into the person God intended you to be.

If you know someone who is a Christian, you could ask them to explain further. You will also need the help of other Christians to begin to live this new life. You will need prayer, teaching, counsel, encouragement, protection, fellowship and so much more that the church can offer. Ask for God's guidance and even though you may not be a Christian yet, if you are sincere, He will find a way to guide you. This is not only my personal experience but that of many other believers too. I cannot emphasise the importance of this step too strongly. Your eternal life hangs in the balance.

The Three Ugly Sisters

The two ugly sisters appear in the story of Cinderella. They hate the fact that Cinderella is beautiful. They keep her in rags and treat her as a servant. But, as we know, there is a wonderful future awaiting Cinderella. She is going to be married to the heir to the throne, dressed in royal robes and seen for the lovely person that she really is, when all is revealed at the end of the story. The ugly sisters will be banished.

We may currently be harassed and harried by the three ugly sisters of covetousness, jealousy, and envy, but we can deal with them with the Lord's help and even turn their attacks to our own advantage; using them to make ourselves more beautiful for the bridegroom.

If you currently feel you are sitting in the cinders, washing the dishes in the bowels of a dark castle, with some wicked presences trying to abuse and dispirit you, I hope a few things in this book will have helped you to cope, and see things differently. It may also help you to know that you are not on you own. That's me, in the other corner of the kitchen, sweeping the floor.

Look up and lift-up your heads, your redemption draws near.

Bibliography

Online resources
Baring-Gould, Sabine. *The Village Pulpit Volume II. Trinity to Advent.* Project Gutenberg
https://biblehub.com/sermons/auth/baring-gould/evil_thoughts.htm
Bible Hub.com https;//biblehub.com/
Spurgeon, Charles. https://www.spurgeon.org/resource-library/sermons/freshness/#flipbook/
https://biblehub.com/sermons/auth/spurgeon/gifts_differ_be_natural.htm
Strong, James. *Strong's Exhaustive Concordance of the Bible.* Abingdon Press 1890
https://biblehub.com/greek/4124.htm
https://biblehub.com/greek/4190.htm

www.ingramcontent.com/pod-product-compliance
Lightning Source LLC
Chambersburg PA
CBHW070915160426
43193CB00011B/1467